# Best Easy Day Hikes
# Canyonlands and Arches National Parks

## Help Us Keep This Guide Up to Date

Every effort has been made by the authors and editors to make this guide as accurate and useful as possible. However, many things can change after a guide is published—trails are rerouted, regulations change, facilities come under new management, etc.

We would love to hear from you concerning your experiences with this guide and how you feel it could be improved and kept up to date. While we may not be able to respond to all comments and suggestions, we'll take them to heart and we'll also make certain to share them with the authors. Please send your comments and suggestions to falconeditorial@rowman.com.

Thanks for your input, and happy trails!

Best Easy Day Hikes Series

# Best Easy Day Hikes Canyonlands and Arches National Parks

Fifth Edition

## Bill Schneider

Published in Partnership with the National
Park Service and the Canyonlands
Natural History Association

## FALCONGUIDES

ESSEX, CONNECTICUT

**FALCON**GUIDES®

An imprint of Globe Pequot, the trade division of The Rowman & Littlefield Publishing Group, Inc.
4501 Forbes Blvd., Ste. 200
Lanham, MD 20706
www.rowman.com

Falcon and FalconGuides are registered trademarks and Make Adventure Your Story is a trademark of The Rowman & Littlefield Publishing Group, Inc.

Distributed by NATIONAL BOOK NETWORK

Maps by Melissa Baker and The Rowman & Littlefield Publishing Group, Inc.

British Library Cataloguing-in-Publication Information available

**Library of Congress Cataloging-in-Publication Data available**

ISBN 978-1-4930-6730-5 (paper: alk. paper)
ISBN 978-1-4930-6731-2 (electronic)

∞™ The paper used in this publication meets the minimum requirements of American National Standard for Information Sciences—Permanence of Paper for Printed Library Materials, ANSI/NISO Z39.48-1992.

# Contents

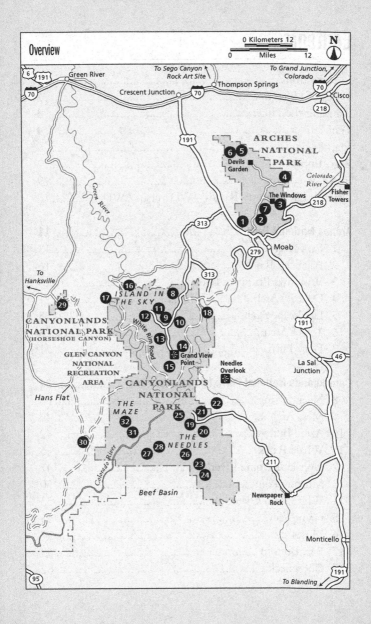

# Introduction

The area encompassed by Arches and Canyonlands National Parks, two scenic gems tucked away in the corner of southeastern Utah, is a big place. And for the hiker, including the beginner, both parks have a lot to offer.

## What's a "Best Easy" Hike?

While researching and writing a much larger book about this area called *Hiking Canyonlands and Arches National Parks,* I had frequent discussions with rangers on what kind of information hikers most requested. I had the same discussions with many hikers out on the trails.

It seems that there are at least two general types of visitors—those who want to spend several days experiencing the depth of the Canyonlands backcountry and those who only have a day or two and would like a choice sampling of the special features of the Canyonlands. This book is primarily for the second group.

The more comprehensive book, *Hiking Canyonlands and Arches,* covers every trail and backcountry road in both parks, including those that are neither best nor easy. *Best Easy Day Hikes* includes only shorter, less strenuous hikes that are my recommendations for the nicest day hikes in these parks.

These hikes vary in length, but most are short. With the exception of the hike to the Great Gallery, none have seriously big hills. (The Great Gallery is such a great hike that I decided to include it even though it has one steep climb.) All hikes are on easy-to-follow trails with no off-trail sections. In some cases, however, it isn't easy to get to the trailhead. You need a high-clearance, four-wheel-drive (4WD) vehicle with low-range gearing and the skill and experience to use it to reach the trailheads for hikes to the Joint Trail, Chesler Park Loop, Devils Pocket Loop, Moses, Spanish Bottom, and the Granary.

Some of the hikes in this book might not seem easy to some but will be easy to others. To help you decide, I've ranked the hikes from easiest to hardest. Please keep in mind that short does not always equal easy. Other factors such as elevation gain and trail conditions have to be considered. Also, in Canyon Country, the midsummer heat can make any hike difficult.

Enjoy the "best easy" hiking in wonderful Canyonlands and Arches National Parks.

# Types of Hikes

The suggested hikes in this book have been split into the following categories:

Loop—Starts and finishes at the trailhead, with no (or very little) retracing of your steps, including "lollipop" loops with part of the route out-and-back on the same trail.

Shuttle—A point-to-point trip that requires two vehicles (one left at the other end of the trail) or a prearranged pickup at a designated time and place.

Out-and-back—Traveling to a specific destination, then retracing your steps back to the trailhead.

# Ranking the Hikes

The following list numerically ranks the hikes in this book from easiest (1) to most challenging (32):

# Trail Finder

## Best Hikes for Small Children

## Best Hikes to Arches

## Best Hikes through Canyons

## Best Hikes to Scenic Vistas

# Map Legend

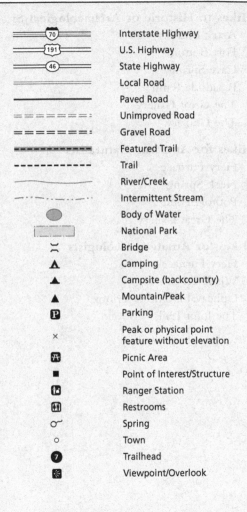

| | |
|---|---|
| —70— | Interstate Highway |
| —191— | U.S. Highway |
| —46— | State Highway |
| | Local Road |
| | Paved Road |
| = = = = = | Unimproved Road |
| = = = = = | Gravel Road |
| ▬▬▬▬▬ | Featured Trail |
| - - - - - | Trail |
| | River/Creek |
| | Intermittent Stream |
| ⬭ | Body of Water |
| ▭ | National Park |
| ≍ | Bridge |
| ▲ | Camping |
| ▲ | Campsite (backcountry) |
| ▲ | Mountain/Peak |
| P | Parking |
| × | Peak or physical point feature without elevation |
| 𐃷 | Picnic Area |
| ■ | Point of Interest/Structure |
| 🏠 | Ranger Station |
| 🚻 | Restrooms |
| ⚲ | Spring |
| ○ | Town |
| 7 | Trailhead |
| ✺ | Viewpoint/Overlook |

# Zero Impact

Going into a national park is like visiting a famous museum. You obviously don't want to leave your mark on an art treasure in the museum. If everybody going through the museum left one little mark, the piece of art would be quickly destroyed—and of what value is a big building full of trashed art? The same goes for pristine wildernesses such as Canyonlands and Arches National Parks, which are as magnificent as any masterpiece by any artist. If we all left just one little mark on the landscape, the wilderness would soon be despoiled.

A wilderness can accommodate a lot of human use if everybody behaves. But a few thoughtless or uninformed visitors can ruin it for everybody who follows. The need for good manners applies to all wilderness users, not just hikers. We all must leave no clues of our passing.

Most of us know better than to litter. Be sure you leave nothing, regardless of how small it is, along the trail or at the campsite. This means you should pack out everything, including orange peels, flip tops, cigarette butts, and gum wrappers. Also pick up trash others left behind.

Follow the main trail. Avoid cutting switchbacks and walking on vegetation beside the trail. In the desert, the terrain can be very fragile, so if possible, stay on the trail. If you're hiking off-trail, try to hike on slickrock or in canyon washes.

Don't pick up "souvenirs," such as rocks, antlers, or wildflowers. The next person wants to see them, too, and collecting such souvenirs violates park regulations.

Avoid making loud noises that may disturb others. Remember, sound travels easily to the other side of the canyon. Be courteous.

Carry a lightweight trowel and bury human waste 6–8 inches deep and pack out used toilet paper. Keep waste at least 300 feet away from any water source.

Finally, and perhaps most important, strictly follow the pack-in/pack-out rule. If you carry something into the back-country, consume it or carry it out.

# Endangered Dirt

Some advocates of zero-impact recreation suggest, "leave only footprints," but in the high desert, this is bad advice. One footprint can destroy decades of growth.

Cryptobiotic crust is the foundation of life in the high desert. It provides a seedbed for the desert plant community and serves as a sponge, retaining the precious moisture of a dry climate. The crust is also the primary source for fixation of nitrogen, which is crucial to all life in the desert. This crust is a complex community of microorganisms, the most important of which are called cyanobacteria.

When mature, cryptobiotic soil has a lumpy, black-tinged crust. In earlier stages, the crust is almost invisible. If you step on it, ride on it, or drive on it, it blows away and erodes, and then it takes many years, if not decades, to recover.

This is a prime reason to stay on trails and roads. If you have to hike off-trail, try to stay on slickrock or in canyon washes to prevent stepping on cryptobiotic crust.

When somebody says, "Watch your step," he or she often has safety in mind, but in Canyonlands, this can mean the preservation of the high desert environment.

# Driving Backcountry Roads: 4WD versus AWD

One persistent problem faced by rangers in Arches and Canyonlands National Parks is visitors who incorrectly believe they have the skills and the vehicle suited for the rough backcountry roads in the parks. There seems to be a common misconception that "All-Wheel-Drive" (AWD) is the same as "Four-Wheel-Drive" (4WD), when it certainly is not. To drive many of these roads, you need a true high-clearance, 4WD vehicle with low-range gearing.

Even if you have the correct vehicle, you need the skills and experience necessary to navigate rough roads. If not, you might be looking at a dangerous and expensive rescue operation. In other words, don't rent a jeep for the first time and assume you can drive these roads.

If you have any doubts about the suitability of your vehicle or the skills required, discuss it with rangers at the visitor centers.

The best source of more information on vehicle requirements is the information-packed National Park Service (NPS) websites. If you can't find what you need there, you can get the information at the following addresses and phone numbers:

Arches National Park
PO Box 907
Moab, UT 84532
Phone: (435) 719-2299
E-mail: archinfo@nps.gov
Website: www.nps.gov/arch

Canyonlands National Park
2282 South West Resource Blvd.
Moab, UT 84532
Phone: (435) 719-2313
E-mail: canyinfo@nps.gov
Website: www.nps.gov/cany

# Arches National Park

Compared to many national parks, Arches is small (73,379 acres), but it's very scenic and very popular. It was designated a national monument in 1929 and then expanded and designated a national park in 1971.

Water, wind, extreme temperatures, and other geologic forces have created the greatest diversity of arches in the world at Arches National Park, along with many other multihued, finely sculpted rock formations. Delicate Arch, perhaps the park's most famous feature, shows up in an endless array of videos, postcards, posters, books, and magazines. However, the numerous arches along the Devils Garden hike, the cathedralesque columns of Park Avenue, the cavernlike canyons of Fiery Furnace, along with many other spectacular features rival the Delicate Arch (and just about everything else in nature!) for awesome beauty.

A hole in a rock has to have an opening of at least 3 feet to be officially listed as an arch and be given a name. Arches National Park has more than 2,000 arches, a preponderance of arches that makes the park unique. In fact, there is no place on Earth even remotely like it.

Arches National Park is not well suited for the serious hiker. Instead, it's better suited for the visitor who doesn't mind seeing most scenery from the car window and on short walks. The trails offer spectacular scenery but, with one exception, all are short day hikes. Unlike Canyonlands National Park, Arches offers limited opportunities to the four-wheeler with only three short backcountry road sections.

The park is open 24 hours a day, 7 days a week. The visitor center is open every day, but hours vary. Check the park's website (www.nps.com/arch) for exact hours.

The park has a fifty-two-site campground at Devils Garden. During the prime season (March through October), camping sites must be reserved online at www.recreation.gov. In the off-season, sites go on a first-come/first-served basis.

In 2022, Arches launched a pilot timed-entry program that required visitors to obtain a ticket from www.recreation.gov months in advance of traveling to Arches. In 2023, the park installed a similar system with only minor changes. If you're planning a trip to Arches, go to the park's website, www.nps.gov/arch, months in advance of your trip for details on the latest timed-entry system and then go to www.recreation.gov, again months in advance of your trip, to obtain your ticket to enter the park. This is a bit of a hassle, to be sure, but with popularity continuing to increase yearly, the park really must manage visitation. Arches only has one entry point and one paved road, and without regulation, it becomes choked with traffic, negatively impacting the experience for all visitors.

## Getting to Arches National Park

Arches National Park is located 25 miles south of I-70 and 5 miles north of Moab on US 191. The starting points for hikes and drives are referenced from the entrance station.

# 1  Park Avenue

A scenic stroll in the shadow of nature's skyscrapers.

**Start:** Park Avenue Parking Area
**Distance:** 1 mile; shuttle

**Maps:** Trails Illustrated Arches National Park and USGS Arches National Park

**Finding the trailhead:** The Park Avenue Parking Area is on your left 2.5 miles from the entrance station. The Courthouse Towers Parking Area is on your right 3.7 miles from the entrance station in the shadow of the massive Courthouse Towers. GPS coordinates: N37 27.653' / W109 35.967'

## The Hike

The Park Avenue Trail is most aptly named for New York City's famous street. Early travelers noticed a similarity between these sandstone spires and the famous skyscrapers along New York's Park Avenue, and the name stuck. The main difference, of course, is that nature, not mankind, sculpted the "skyscrapers" of Arches National Park.

Although you can start at either end of this shuttle trail, starting at the south end results in a totally downhill hike, but the slope is very gradual. However, if you want to arrange your own shuttle (not provided by NPS), start at the north end and have somebody pick you up at the south end. If you don't have access to two vehicles and can't arrange a shuttle, this hike is still definitely worth taking, even with double the mileage (only 2 miles) by going out and back.

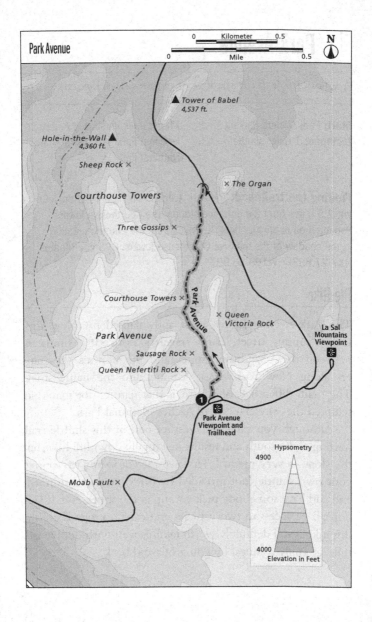

Park Avenue

Kilometer
0                          0.5
Mile
0                          0.5

N

▲ Tower of Babel
4,537 ft.

Hole-in-the-Wall ▲
4,360 ft.

Sheep Rock ×

Courthouse Towers

× The Organ

Three Gossips ×

Courthouse Towers ×

Park Avenue

× Queen
Victoria Rock

La Sal
Mountains
Viewpoint

Sausage Rock ×

Queen Nefertiti Rock ×

❶

Park Avenue
Viewpoint and
Trailhead

Moab Fault ×

Hypsometry

4900

4000

Elevation in Feet

You'll really be missing something if you leave Arches without taking this short hike. You can see the Courthouse Towers, Tower of Babel, Three Gossips, the Organ, and other grand "skyscrapers" from the road, but if you don't take this hike, you'll miss the truly stimulating experience of walking among them.

From the south, the trail starts out as a concrete path leading to a scenic overlook about 100 yards from the trailhead. From here, a well-defined trail goes through juniper and cactus until it melts into a slickrock dry wash, marked by an occasional cairn, and stays there until just before you return to the main road. The trail disappears at times, but there's no chance of getting lost. Stay in the dry wash and follow well-placed cairns to the Courthouse Towers Parking Area.

# 2  Balanced Rock

A very easy walk to the base of a fragile, picturesque rock formation.

**Start:** Balanced Rock Parking Area

**Distance:** 0.3 mile; loop

**Maps:** Trails Illustrated Arches National Park and USGS Arches National Park

**Finding the trailhead:** The Balanced Rock Parking Area is on the east side of the main park road 9 miles from the entrance station. GPS coordinates: N42 06.332' / W109 33.950'

## The Hike

This is a short hike, perfect for travelers who would like to stretch their legs without working up a big sweat. You can see Balanced Rock and read about it on an interpretive display at the parking area, but it's more impressive up close. The trail makes a short loop around Balanced Rock and returns to the parking area.

The forces of nature sculpted Balanced Rock out of Entrada Sandstone. Technically this is called a "caprock" of harder Slick Rock Member (a part of Entrada Sandstone) perched on a pedestal of softer Dewey Bridge Member (a part of the Carmel Formation). The pedestal erodes more quickly than the more resistant caprock. The entire Balanced Rock formation is 128 feet high, and the rock itself measures 55 feet.

Balanced Rock used to have a companion called "Chip Off the Old Block," but it toppled during the winter of 1975–1976. You can still see its pedestal on the south side of Balanced Rock.

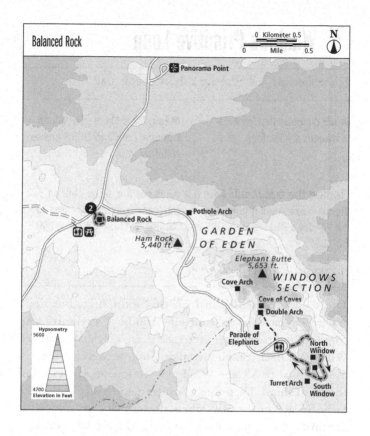

Balanced Rock

0 Kilometer 0.5
0 Mile 0.5

N

Panorama Point

Pothole Arch

2 Balanced Rock

GARDEN
OF EDEN

Ham Rock
5,440 ft.

Elephant Butte
5,653 ft.

Cove Arch

WINDOWS
SECTION

Cove of Caves

Double Arch

Parade of
Elephants

North
Window

Turret Arch

South
Window

Hypsometry
5600

4700
Elevation in Feet

# 3 Windows Primitive Loop

Three fantastic arches along a short, scenic trail.

**Start:** Windows Parking Area  
**Distance:** 1 mile; loop

**Maps:** Trails Illustrated Arches National Park and USGS Arches National Park

**Finding the trailhead:** Drive 9.2 miles north into the park on the main road until it forks. Take a right (east) and drive 3 miles to the Windows Parking Area. GPS coordinates: N41 13.680' / W109 32.183'

## The Hike

The scenery is sensational on this short hike, but don't expect to have it to yourself. Almost everybody who comes to the park hikes up to see these spectacular arches. When you hear somebody talking about overcrowding in the national parks, the Windows section of Arches often comes to mind. Therefore consider taking this short hike early or late in the day when the crowds are somewhat diminished, and you have a better chance of scoring a parking place.

Although it seems like it should be the other way around, the trail goes to the North Window and then to the South Window. On the way to the North Window, take a short side trip to the right (south) to see Turret Arch. The Windows are sometimes called the Spectacles, and you can see why. If you hike the primitive loop around the back of the arches, you can see the "nose" on which the spectacles rest.

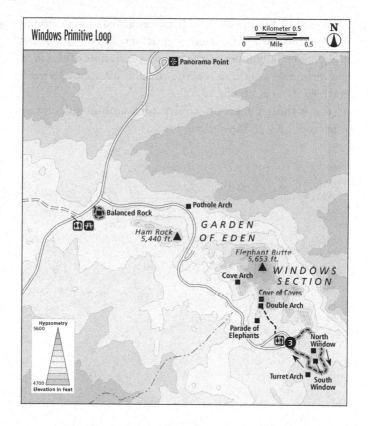

It's fairly easy to go off-trail and climb up right under North Window and Turret Arch. Do not attempt to climb into South Window. Several people have fallen while trying or have gotten stranded here. Be careful not to fall or damage any vegetation or natural features. Also, hang onto your hat. The strong winds in the area tend to blow it off as soon as you reach either arch.

After you finish marveling at the Windows and Turret Arch, continue along the well-defined loop trail from the viewpoint of South Window. It makes a small circle around the Windows, giving you another great view of North Window. It also offers a glimpse at the native vegetation of the area. The primitive loop trail hits the parking lot about 50 yards north of the main trailhead.

For a shorter hike (0.7 mile), turn around and retrace your steps back to the parking lot.

# $4$ **Delicate Arch**

A moderately difficult and very heavily used route to the world's most famous arch.

**Start:** Wolfe Ranch Parking Area
**Distance:** 3 miles; out-and-back

**Maps:** Trails Illustrated Arches National Park and USGS Arches National Park

**Finding the trailhead:** Drive 11.7 miles north into the park on the main road until you see the right-hand turn to Delicate Arch and Wolfe Ranch. Turn right and drive another 1.2 miles to the parking area on your left (north). Look to your right for a lot for oversize vehicles. GPS coordinates: N44 07.703' / W109 31.233'

## The Hike

If you've ever seen a postcard or poster of Arches National Park, you've probably seen Delicate Arch. This amazing arch has become the symbol of Arches National Park, which is somewhat surprising because it's barely visible from the road.

Try to get here early. The temperature will be more pleasant, and you might even find a parking spot. The trailhead has a Walmart-sized parking lot, but it's often full after 9 a.m.

You have three options for viewing this magnificent natural feature. You can take a 1.5-mile trail (3 miles round-trip), which goes right under the arch; you can go to the Delicate Arch Viewpoint; or you can take a 5-minute walk to a closer viewpoint. If you choose the hiking option, be aware that the trail to Delicate Arch is not a stroll. This is a real hike, and you should be prepared. Bring extra water, wear good hiking shoes, and try to avoid the midday heat. You're often walking on slickrock following cairns much of the way, and there's little shade along the way. The NPS describes the trail as "strenuous," and it truly can be for the inexperienced, poorly conditioned hiker, especially on a hot summer day. So be prepared.

If you decide to see the famous arch from the viewpoint instead of taking the hike, you have to keep driving past the Wolfe Ranch Trailhead for another 1.2 miles to the Delicate Arch Viewpoint Parking Area.

At the Wolfe Ranch Trailhead, you can see the remains of the historic Wolfe Ranch, settled in 1888 and sold by John Wolfe in 1910. Shortly after leaving the trailhead, you cross over Salt Wash on a sturdy new bridge. Right after the bridge, you might notice a large pile of "green stuff" on your right. This is volcanic ash with a high iron content that has gone through a chemical process that gives it this greenish cast.

Just after the bridge, you can take a short side trip to the left to a Ute petroglyph panel. This is well worth adding a quarter mile to your trip.

During the first part of the hike, watch for collared lizards. These large lizards can run on their hind feet when chasing prey.

For the first half mile or so, you hike on a wide, well-defined, mostly level trail, probably the best trail you've ever been on. Then the excellent trail disappears, and you start a gradual ascent to Delicate Arch. Most of the rest of the trip is on slickrock, so be alert. You have to follow cairns and a few strategically located signs the rest of the way, and sometimes the "cairns" are only one rock. Don't worry about getting lost. You can almost always see a string of hikers ahead of you.

As you get closer to Delicate Arch, you can see Frame Arch off to your right (south). This arch forms a perfect "frame" for

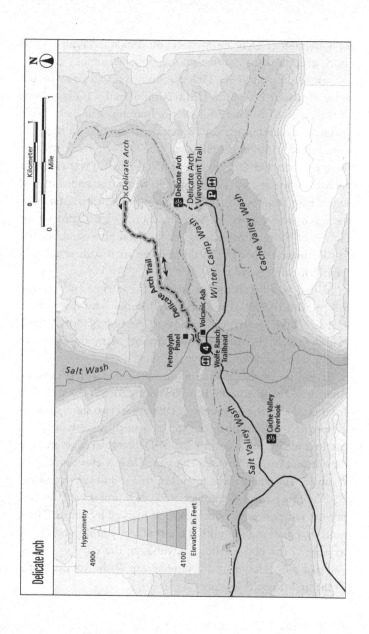

Delicate Arch

a photograph of Delicate Arch. If you decide to climb up this short, steep slope to get that photograph, be careful.

Just before you get to Delicate Arch, the trail goes along a ledge for about 200 yards. This section of trail was blasted out of the cliff, and you can still see the bore holes in the rock. If you have children with you, watch them carefully in this section. Just after the ledge ends, you see Delicate Arch with its huge opening (33 feet wide and 45 feet high). You can take an awe-inspiring walk down to right below the arch, but you might ruin somebody's photo. A shot of Delicate Arch with the often-snowcapped La Sal Mountains as a backdrop must be one of those photos every professional photographer has to have in his or her file, so shutterbugs are usually setting up tripods for the grand view.

When you finally come around the corner and see the full breadth of Delicate Arch, you'll know why this is such a classic hike, perhaps the best in Arches National Park. And definitely one of the most popular. Many thousands of people take this hike every year.

If you prefer the less strenuous option for seeing Delicate Arch, drive past the Wolfe Ranch Parking Area and go another 1.2 miles. From the parking area, take one of two short walks—a short (0.5-mile) trail to the top of a small ridge where you can look north for a good view of Delicate Arch, or an even shorter trail to a different viewpoint. These views don't quite compare with being right there, but they're still awe-inspiring.

The first part of the longer viewpoint trail is well defined, but the last part goes over slickrock marked by cairns. There is no sign marking the end of the trail, but you'll know when to stop. At the end of the trail, you're at the edge of a steep cliff that drops down into Winter Camp Wash. You can't hike to the arch from this point.

# 5 Landscape Arch

A short stroll to the longest arch in the park, plus a short side trip to two more large arches.

**Start:** Devils Garden Trailhead Parking Area
**Distance:** 1.6 miles; out-and-back

**Maps:** Trails Illustrated Arches National Park and USGS Arches National Park

**Finding the trailhead:** Drive north into the park on the main road for 19 miles and park in the large parking area at the Devils Garden Trailhead. The trailhead is at the end of the road where it makes a small loop. Be sure to stay on the loop instead of turning into the Devils Garden Campground. GPS coordinates: N46 58.354' / W109 35.683'

## The Hike

The hike to Landscape Arch is akin to the trip to Delicate Arch. It's one of those must-see features of Arches National Park.

Landscape Arch has an opening spanning an incredible 306 feet, which may make it the longest stone span in the world. On the geologic time scale, Landscape Arch is a senior citizen among arches in the park. It's also famous for the extreme slenderness of its stone span.

And don't wait too long to see it. Geologically speaking, it's likely to collapse any day.

This is a "super trail"—flat, easy, double-wide all the way, and usually heavily populated with hikers.

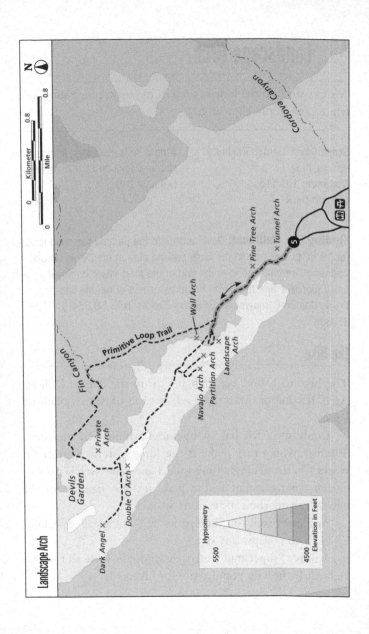

Landscape Arch

Dark Angel ×

Devils Garden

Double O Arch ×

Fin Canyon

× Private Arch

Primitive Loop Trail

Wall Arch

Navajo Arch ×

Partition Arch ×

Landscape Arch

Pine Tree Arch ×

× Tunnel Arch

Cordova Canyon

N

Kilometer    0    0.8

Mile    0    0.8

Hypsometry

Elevation in Feet

5500    4500

About a quarter mile from the trailhead, the trail splits. To go to Landscape Arch, take the left-hand fork. The right-hand fork takes you on a short spur trail down to Pine Tree and Tunnel Arches, both well worth adding 0.4 mile to your hike. If you take this spur trail, it splits again at the bottom of a small hill. Go left to Pine Tree Arch and right to Tunnel Arch. After checking out these two large arches, head back to the main trail and on to Landscape Arch.

Just before you see Landscape Arch and as you descend a series of steps, you come to the junction with the Devils Garden Primitive Loop Trail. Stay left here, and continue for about another quarter mile for your chance to marvel at the incredible Landscape Arch.

# 6 Tower Arch

A moderate hike to one of the most remote arches in the park.

**Start:** Tower Arch Trailhead
**Distance:** 3.4 miles; out-and-back

**Maps:** Trails Illustrated Arches National Park and USGS Arches National Park

**Finding the trailhead:** Turn left (west) onto Salt Valley Road, which leaves the main road 16 miles beyond the entrance station. You can take any vehicle on this road, but the NPS recommends staying off it when it's wet, so don't get caught in a thunderstorm. Follow the road for 7.1 miles until you see a junction with a sign pointing to a left turn to Klondike Bluffs. Take this road for 1.1 miles until it ends at the Tower Arch Trailhead. At this junction, be sure to take the second left turn to Klondike Bluffs Road, not the first left, a primitive 4WD road to Balanced Rock. GPS coordinates: N47 32.780' / W109 40.500'

## The Hike

Tower Arch is a short but rugged hike, or as indicated by the sign at the trailhead, a primitive trail, and the NPS considers it "strenuous." To avoid an afternoon thunderstorm, which makes the Salt Valley Road impassable, start early.

The trail immediately starts to climb to the top of the bluff, up a steep but short incline. After this brief climb, the trail continues up and down until you see the massive Tower Arch surrounded by a maze of spectacular sandstone spires. Along the way, you get great views of the Marching Men rock formation on your left and the austere Klondike Bluffs on your right.

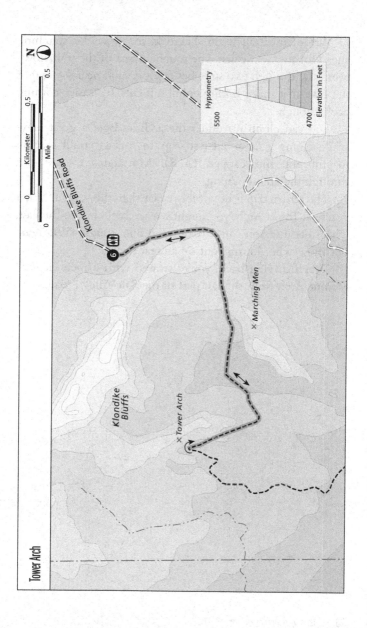

Tower Arch

N

Klondike Bluffs Road

Klondike Bluffs

× Tower Arch

× Marching Men

Hypsometry

5500    4700

Elevation in Feet

Kilometer
0        0.5

Mile
0        0.5

Part of the trail is on slickrock, so always be watching ahead for the next cairn. The roughest part of the trail, however, goes through two stretches of loose sand near the end of the hike that make hiking uphill difficult. It's easier coming back, though.

You can climb up under the arch and get a great view while taking a deserved rest stop. In spring, you'll see the magnificent, snowcapped La Sal Mountains to the east through the arch opening.

The return trip is noticeably easier than the way in. When you're at Tower Arch, you might see a vehicle just to the east. That's because you can drive around on a rough 4WD road, but those who do miss out on a great hike.

When driving back, you're treated with a nice view of Skyline Arch from the last part of the Salt Valley Road.

# 7  Fiery Furnace

A ranger-guided tour of a rare desert environment.

**Start:** Fiery Furnace Parking Area
**Distance:** 2 miles; loop

**Maps:** Trails Illustrated Arches National Park and USGS Arches National Park

**Finding the trailhead:** Drive north into the park on the main road for 14.5 miles and turn right (east) at the well-signed Fiery Furnace Road (just after the Salt Valley Overlook). Park in the Fiery Furnace Parking Area, which is a short drive from the main road. GPS coordinates: N44 34.544' / W109 33.933'

## The Hike

To see the Fiery Furnace area of Arches National Park, you can take a ranger-led tour. You can explore the area by yourself with a hiking permit obtained at the park's visitor center, but I highly recommend signing up for the guided tour, where you'll learn ten times more than you would on your own, and you won't get lost. Also, you will have much less impact on this fragile desert environment.

You can reserve a spot in the morning tours through Recreation.gov, but for afternoon tours and for tours anytime during the shoulder seasons, you have to sign up in person at the visitor center. Because of the rough terrain, the NPS only allows hikers over 5 years of age. For current information on Fiery Furnace tours, follow the links on the park's website: www.nps.gov/arch.

The Fiery Furnace isn't named for its average temperature. Actually, it belies its name and remains fairly cool even in midsummer due to the many shady canyons. Instead, the area was named for the reddish glow it often takes on at sunset, which resembles a furnace.

After a brief orientation talk, a ranger leads the guided tour down one of the faint trails leaving the parking area. Three hours later, you return to the parking area on another trail. As you walk along the 2-mile loop, the ranger explains the incredible natural history of the area and points out rare plants and semi-concealed arches. As with any desert hike, be sure to take water.

The Fiery Furnace has suffered from its popularity. As a result, the NPS imposed special restrictions in 1994 in an attempt to curb a disturbing amount of damage to the fragile resources of the area. If you elect to go exploring on your own, you must talk to a ranger, who will help you understand the problems of overuse and discuss getting a permit. The area is a labyrinth of narrow sandstone canyons, and there are no marked trails, making it difficult to stay oriented.

Two defined trails leave the trailhead, but they soon melt away into a fascinating puzzle of crevasses, fins, and boulders. This maze of canyons may be one of the most difficult areas to hike in the park, but it's also one of the most remarkable. The scenery, especially the steep-sided canyons and weird-shaped rocks, along with several arches and bridges, is unforgettable. You can also find a totally quiet place in the Fiery Furnace to help you forget the stress in your life.

The Fiery Furnace also provides critical habitat for many rare plant species, such as the Canyonlands biscuitroot, so please be intensely careful not to step on black-crusted cryptobiotic soil (desert topsoil) or delicate plant communities. Try to walk on rock or in sandy washes.

The NPS charges a nominal fee for both ranger-led tours and permits in the Fiery Furnace area.

Because of sensitive and threatened vegetation and the fact that it's easy to get lost in this area, the NPS prefers that no map of the route be included with this hike description.

# Canyonlands National Park: Island in the Sky

I sland in the Sky is a high mesa wedged between the Colorado and Green Rivers like a natural observation platform. Vistas rival those found anywhere. This district of Canyonlands National Park is also the darling of the mountain biker, and mountain-biking tours on the White Rim Road have become intensely popular. During peak seasons, campsites along the road are always full, having been reserved many months in advance. The NPS has long required backcountry permits for overnight stays on the White Rim Road, but now, the agency also requires permits for day use.

However, those without a mountain bike need not worry. Island in the Sky has lots to offer hikers. The trail system is not as extensive as the Needles District, but hikers may choose from a variety of well-maintained trails. Trails dropping off the mesa and going to the White Rim Road are for the serious hiker, but the area also has easy and moderate hiking opportunities.

Many four-wheelers enjoy the White Rim Road (day-use permit required) and side roads, but these roads might not present a serious challenge for experts. Tourists with only a day or two to spend here can view some fantastic scenery from the main paved roads in the park. They can supplement their brief visit with several excellent short hikes on the mesa

(Grand View, White Rim Overlook, Mesa Arch, Aztec Butte, Whale Rock, or Upheaval Dome Overlook).

Rangers at the Island in the Sky visitor center (on your right about a mile past the entrance station) can answer your questions about the natural features and recreational opportunities found in the Island in the Sky District of Canyonlands National Park.

## Getting to Island in the Sky

From Moab drive 10 miles north on US 191 to SR 313. To reach the same point from farther north, drive 22 miles south from I-70. Once on SR 313, drive southwest 25 miles to the Island in the Sky entrance station.

# 8  Neck Spring

A popular day hike and one of the few loop routes in Island in the Sky.

**Start:** Neck Spring Trailhead at Shafer Canyon Overlook
**Distance:** 6 miles; loop

**Maps:** Trails Illustrated Island in the Sky and USGS Musselman Arch

**Finding the trailhead:** Drive 0.2 mile south of the Island in the Sky visitor center and turn left (east) into the Shafer Canyon Overlook Parking Area. GPS coordinates: N27 08.626' / W109 49.217'

## The Hike

The Neck has historical significance. Here the Island in the Sky plateau narrows to about 40 feet with sheer cliffs dropping off on both sides. This natural phenomenon allowed early ranchers who ran livestock in the area (before the park was created) to control the entire 43-square-mile mesa with one 40-foot fence across this narrow spot, later named the Neck. Nature is also making a play at the Neck. Erosion is gradually wearing away the already narrow entrance to Island in the Sky. Sometime in the future, Island in the Sky might really be an island.

The Neck Spring Trail is one of the few loops in the Island in the Sky where most trails are out-and-backs or shuttles. This trail description follows the counterclockwise route. For more information, you can get a small brochure on the Neck Spring area at the visitor center.

For hikers looking for a moderate, half-day hike, this trail is ideal. It's well defined the entire way, with good footing (only a few small slickrock sections) and minor elevation gain. There are a few confusing spots where social trails can be as defined as the main trail, but the main trail is always marked with cairns. Parts of the trail parallel the main road, but you're far enough away that you hardly notice. You will notice, however, the panoramic views from the trail.

The Neck Spring area allows hikers to experience a wide variety of high desert habitats in a small area. In spring, the area often turns into a wildflower garden, so wildflower buffs will love this trail.

After leaving the trailhead, immediately cross the main road and continue on the trail on the other side of the highway. The first part of the trail is actually an old road built by ranchers who used Neck Spring as a water source. Along this section of trail, you'll notice signs of past ranching activities, such as pipes and water troughs.

The trail then drops down in elevation and angles to the left toward Neck Spring, but not directly to the spring. You can easily see it, however. It's tempting to bushwhack over to the spring, but please enjoy it from a distance. This trail gets heavy use, and this is an extremely fragile area.

From the trail, you'll notice a change in the vegetation with species such as Gambel oak and maidenhair fern able to exist in this area with its extra moisture and shade. Also watch for hummingbirds, deer, and other wild animals frequenting the area.

After Neck Spring, the trail climbs slightly as you head toward the second major water source in the area, Cabin Spring. At this spring, you see the same type of vegetative change as Neck Spring—and a few aging signs of past ranching activity. Shortly after Cabin Spring, you face a short but steep climb up to the Island in the Sky mesa. The trail gets

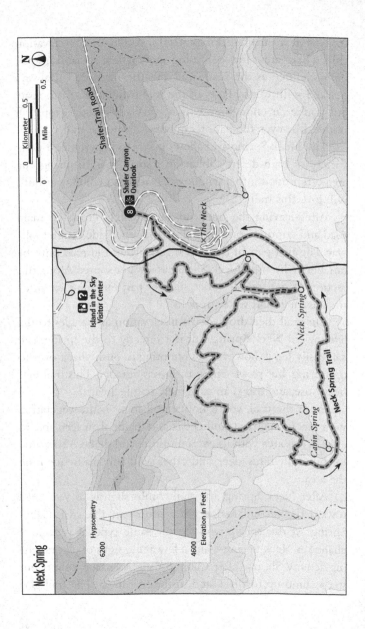

Neck Spring

a little rough here, some of it on slickrock. At the top, you get a grand vista of Upper Taylor Canyon and the Henry Mountains off in the distance.

The last part of the trail follows the rim of the plateau directly above Cabin and Neck Springs and through Gray's Pasture, a grassy bench used for cattle grazing until 1975. With no livestock grazing, the area's native grasses have begun to recover and now provide food for native species only. After passing by the top of Neck Spring, cross the main road again and follow the old roadcut about a half mile back to the parking area. Be careful crossing and walking along the road.

# ⑨ Mesa Arch

A very short walk to a magnificent arch with a spectacular view.

**Start:** Mesa Arch Trailhead
**Distance:** 0.5 mile; loop

**Maps:** Trails Illustrated Island in the Sky and USGS Musselman Arch

**Finding the trailhead:** Drive 6.3 miles south of the Island in the Sky visitor center and turn left (east) into the Mesa Arch Parking Area. GPS coordinates: N23 21.028' / W109 52.083'

## The Hike

This is a perfect trail for beginners. It's easy and short, and a detailed display at the trailhead explains how to hike the trail. Although the NPS manages this trail for beginners, it has something for everybody, and halfway along the short loop you're treated to the spectacular Mesa Arch. The arch is right on the edge of a 500-foot cliff, part of a 1,200-foot drop into Buck Canyon. You can get a keyhole view of the White Rim country through the arch. If you step back a few steps, you can also frame the lofty La Sal Mountains (usually snow-topped in the spring) within the arch.

The trail is well-marked and partly on slickrock. It's an easy hike, but if you have children along, watch them carefully around the arch. There is no fence to prevent a sure-to-be-fatal fall. Do not climb on the arch.

If you look carefully, you can also see another arch from Mesa Arch Overlook—Washer Woman Arch—off to the left (east) when facing the arch.

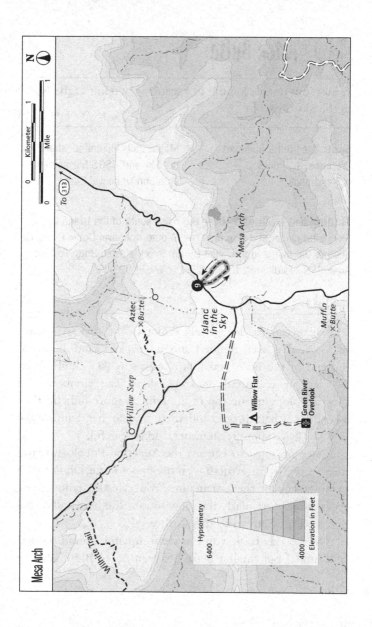

Mesa Arch

# 10 Aztec Butte

A short but not easy climb to a scenic viewpoint of the Island in the Sky area.

**Start:** Aztec Butte Trailhead
**Distance:** 1.2 miles; out-and-back

**Maps:** Trails Illustrated Island in the Sky and USGS Musselman Arch and Upheaval Dome

**Finding the trailhead:** Drive 6.5 miles south of the Island in the Sky visitor center and turn right (west) onto Upheaval Dome Road. Go another 0.8 mile and turn right (north) into the Aztec Butte Parking Area. GPS coordinates: N23 36.581' / W109 52.917'

## The Hike

This hike can be deceptively difficult. The first two-thirds of the trail is well defined and on packed sand, but near the end of the hike, you follow cairns as you climb about 200 feet up a difficult slickrock slope. The climb up the slickrock slope to the top of the butte is more difficult than ascending Whale Rock, and there are no handrails. Make sure you have appropriate shoes, and be careful.

Once on top you can see the Ancestral Puebloan structure—a two-room structure on the upper butte. Don't touch or enter any of these structures. You can also enjoy some great vistas, particularly the view toward the headwall of the massive Trail Canyon to the northwest.

On the way back, you can climb up and around the top of a similar but smaller butte between Aztec Butte and the

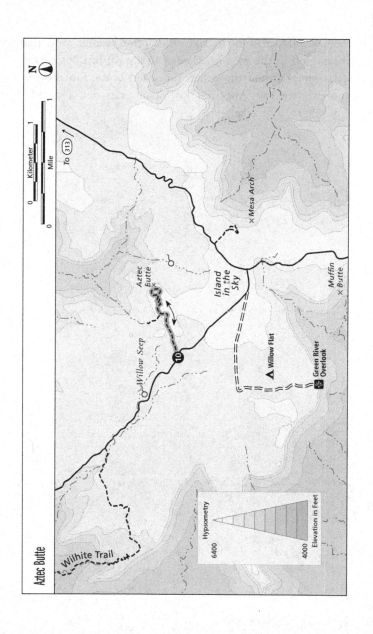

trailhead. If you want to take this option, watch for a trail veering off to the west (marked with a sign) just before you start going around the other, unnamed butte. On the top, you can see two Ancestral Puebloan granaries. This adds 0.8 mile to your hike.

# 11 Whale Rock

A short climb onto one of the most prominent features in the Island in the Sky.

**Start:** Whale Rock Trailhead
**Distance:** 1 mile; out-and-back

**Maps:** Trails Illustrated Island in the Sky and USGS Upheaval Dome

**Finding the trailhead:** Drive 6.5 miles south of the Island in the Sky visitor center and turn right (west) onto Upheaval Dome Road. Go another 3.9 miles to the Whale Rock Parking Area at the trailhead sign on the right (north) side of the road. GPS coordinates: N25 36.566' / W109 54.817'

## The Hike

If you want a great view of the entire Island in the Sky area, take the short climb to the top of Whale Rock. From there you get a 360-degree panoramic look at the entire region. Plan on spending some extra time at the top to study all the interesting geological formations.

The trail goes over slickrock most of the way, but it's carefully marked with cairns. And yes, if you use a little imagination, this rocky outcrop sort of resembles a big whale.

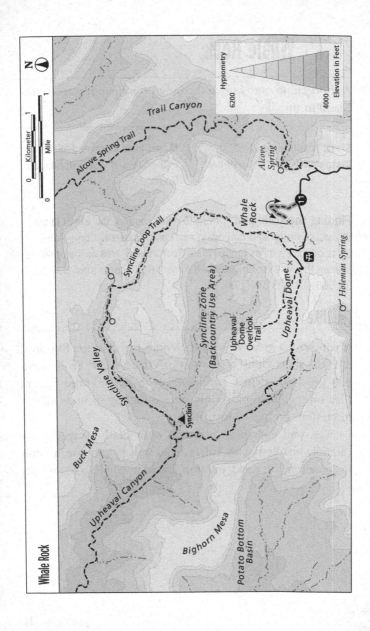

# 12  Upheaval Dome Overlook

A short, steep hike to get the best view of perhaps the most interesting geological feature in Utah.

**Start:** Upheaval Dome Parking Area
**Distance:** 1.6 miles; out-and-back

**Maps:** Trails Illustrated Island in the Sky and USGS Upheaval Dome

**Finding the trailhead:** Drive 6.5 miles south of the Island in the Sky visitor center and turn right (west) onto Upheaval Dome Road. Go another 4.8 miles to the Upheaval Dome Picnic Area at the end of the road. The trailhead is at the west end of the picnic area. GPS coordinates: N25 34.733' / W109 55.550'

## The Hike

This is a great way to observe and study the geological wonders of the Upheaval Dome area without taking the arduous 8.3-mile Syncline Loop. In fact, you get a better view of the mysterious crater from this short trail.

The entire Syncline area has a fascinating—and controversial—geological history. Some geologists call Upheaval Dome "the most peculiar structural feature in southeastern Utah." The origin of the dome is the source of endless debate. For some mysterious reason, rocks formerly buried a mile underground are now on the surface of the crater. The two most common theories—the "salt dome" theory and the "meteorite impact" theory—are explained in a brochure available at the visitor center.

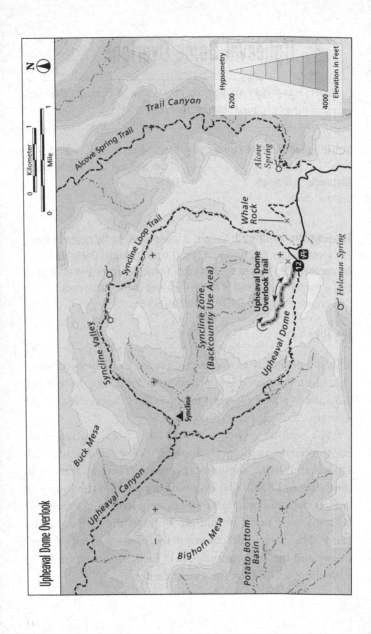

## Upheaval Dome Overlook

Trail Canyon

Alcove Spring Trail

N

Syncline Loop Trail

0          Kilometer          1

0          Mile          1

Whale Rock

Alcove Spring

Syncline Valley

Syncline Zone
(Backcountry Use Area)

Upheaval Dome Overlook Trail

Holeman Spring

Buck Mesa

Syncline

Upheaval Canyon

Upheaval Dome

Hypsometry

6200

4000

Elevation in Feet

Bighorn Mesa

Potato Bottom Basin

About 100 yards up the trail from the parking lot, the loop trail breaks off to the left and right. Continue straight and climb, often on slickrock, for 0.3 mile to the first scenic viewpoint and an excellent interpretive display explaining the famous geology of the area.

The trail continues another 0.5 mile to a second slickrock viewpoint that gives you an even better look at the Upheaval Dome area. This increases the total length of the trip to 1.6 miles, but the hike between the first and second overlooks is only a gradual upgrade. The second outlook is fenced for your protection.

# 13 Murphy Point

An easy, flat day hike or very easy overnighter with a stunning view.

**Start:** Murphy Trailhead
**Distance:** 3.6 miles;
out-and-back

**Maps:** Trails Illustrated Island in the Sky and USGS Monument Basin and Turks Head

**Finding the trailhead:** Drive 8.6 miles south from the Island in the Sky visitor center and park at the pullout at the Murphy Trailhead. GPS coordinates: N21 17.993' / W109 51.817'

## The Hike

The Murphy Point Trail used to be Murphy Point Road, which went to within 0.2 mile of the overlook. In 1996 the NPS converted most of the road to a trail starting at the Murphy Trailhead. (Some older maps may still show it as a road.) This created a nice hike with an absolutely stunning view.

The trail is mostly flat as it stays on the same level as Island in the Sky. Because you're walking on what used to be a two-wheel-drive road, it's easy going. About 0.2 mile from the point, the trail reaches the spot where vehicles used to park. The rest of the way is on an easy trail with some slickrock sections.

From the point, you get a breathtaking view of the White Rim country west of Island in the Sky, including the Green River slowly making its way to a grand meeting with the Colorado River a few miles later. Junction Butte dominates the southern horizon. You can see White Rim Road curving

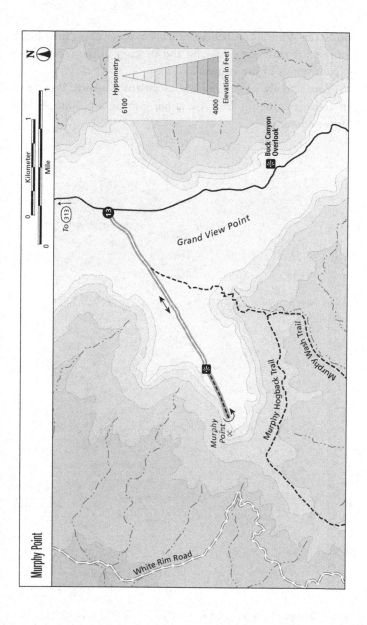

Murphy Point

N

Hypsometry

Elevation in Feet
6100     4000

Kilometer
0     1
Mile
0     1

To 313

13

Grand View Point

Buck Canyon Overlook

Murphy Point
×

Murphy Hogback Trail

Murphy Wash Trail

White Rim Road

along the White Rim Sandstone far below. Plan on spending some extra time here relaxing and soaking in the incredible expansiveness of the canyonlands.

You actually can spend the night on Murphy Point in an at-large camping area. Ask about getting a permit at the visitor center.

# 14 White Rim Overlook

A short, flat walk with a great view of White Rim country.

**Start:** Island in the Sky Picnic Area, White Rim Lookout Trailhead
**Distance:** 1.8 miles; out-and-back

**Maps:** Trails Illustrated Island in the Sky and USGS Monument Basin

**Finding the trailhead:** Drive 11.2 miles south from the Island in the Sky visitor center and turn left (east) into the picnic area. There is no trailhead sign on the main road. GPS coordinates: N19 22.274' / W109 50.967'

## The Hike

You can get a good view of the White Rim area from the parking lot, but a short enjoyable walk gives you a really good view. The White Rim Overlook Trail starts at the right (south) side of the parking lot. It's flat and easy to follow the entire way. Some sections rely on well-placed cairns to show the way.

The trail ends at the end of a peninsula jutting out to the east from the Island in the Sky mesa. From the end of the trail, you can soak in an incredible panoramic view of the entire area. If it's near lunchtime, bring along a snack and a drink and have your lunch surrounded by the quiet beauty of the high desert before heading back to the parking lot.

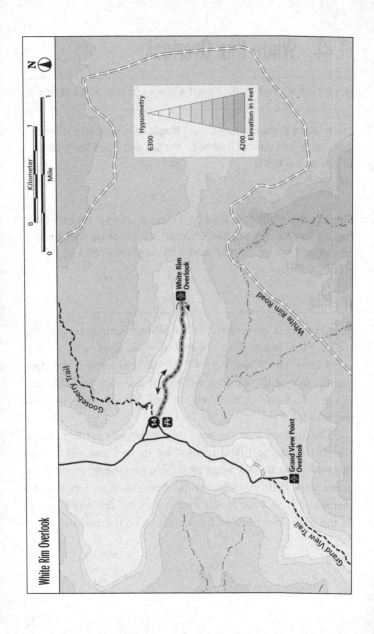

# 15  Grand View

An easy day hike with a well-named view.

**Start:** Grand View Point Overlook
**Distance:** 2 miles; out-and-back

**Maps:** Trails Illustrated Island in the Sky and USGS Monument Basin

**Finding the trailhead:** Drive south from the Island in the Sky visitor center for 12 miles all the way to the end of the main road. GPS coordinates: N18 38.702' / E 109 51.383'

## The Hike

The NPS has placed several wonderful interpretive signs at the Grand View Trailhead, including a panoramic sign that names many of the prominent features in the area such as the Totem Pole, the confluence of the Colorado and Green Rivers, and the White Rim Road winding its way around Island in the Sky.

This trail is flat all the way but poorly defined in spots, with lots of cairns showing the way. Be careful not to get too close to the cliffs. It's a long way down. If you have small children, watch them carefully.

At the end of the trail, you can sit and absorb a truly grand view, contemplating how nature transformed what was formerly a featureless plain into what you see today.

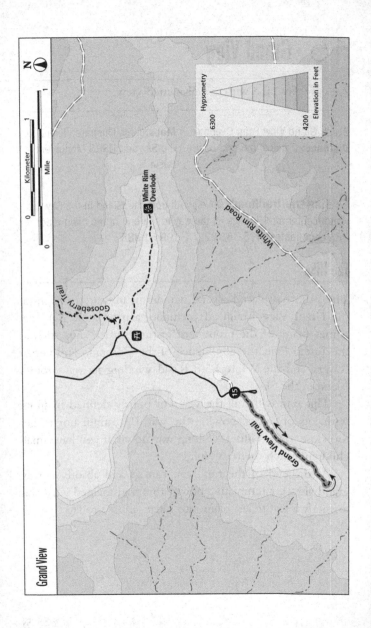

# 16 Moses

A route developed by climbers for some of their favorite climbs, but also a nice hike for nonclimbers.

**Start:** End of Taylor Canyon Road
**Distance:** 2 miles; lollipop loop

**Maps:** Trails Illustrated Island in the Sky and USGS Upheaval Dome

**Finding the trailhead:** You need a 4WD vehicle to reach this trailhead. To find the Taylor Canyon Road, get on the White Rim Road, which turns off SR 313, 6.4 miles north of the Island in the Sky Entrance Station. Drive 18.2 miles to the park boundary and then another 2.5 miles to the junction with the Taylor Canyon Road. Turn left (east) and drive to the end of Taylor Canyon Road, park in the parking area, and walk less than a quarter mile east to the point where both the Moses Trail and the Alcove Spring Trail start and end. GPS coordinates: N28 30.450' / W109 55.133'

## The Hike

This trail climbs up and around the Zeus and Moses spires and then goes through the little pass between Moses and a smaller spire called Aphrodite (unnamed on the maps), all darlings of the rock-climbing fraternity. The route gets you up close and personal to these awe-inspiring formations.

It's a healthy climb to the base of the formations. Use caution hiking the loop around them, but if you start thinking this is risky, think of the people who climb all the way to the top. They make the official trail seem like a mall walk.

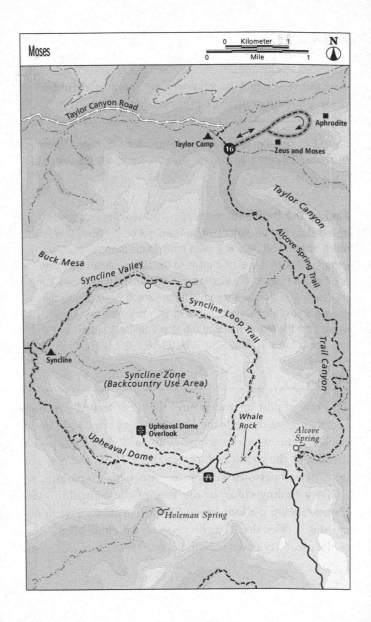

# 17 Fort Bottom

A day hike through the recent and not-so-recent history of the region.

**Start:** Fort Bottom Trailhead
**Distance:** 3 miles to the ruin or 4 miles to the cabin; out-and-back

**Maps:** Trails Illustrated Island in the Sky and USGS Horsethief Canyon

**Finding the trailhead:** From the entrance station, drive White Rim Road in your high-clearance, 4WD vehicle for 66.1 miles and park at the parking area on the left (west) side of the road. You can also reach the trailhead from the north, 6.1 miles from the park boundary, if you have a 4WD vehicle. GPS coordinates: N26 39.009' / W110 01.050'

## The Hike

This interesting hike has two destinations. You can hike down to the bottomland where an old ranch building sits (a 4-mile round-trip), or you can climb up to the top of a small butte (3 miles out-and-back) to check out an intriguing structure built by Ancestral Puebloans.

The first part of the trail is a recently abandoned road, so it's very easy walking. About a mile from the trailhead, you go over a little divide made out of bentonite clay and then around the north side of the butte. Once on the other side, you can take a short side trip by taking a left at a junction you'll find there and climb up to the ruin (which you could see on the way down). After checking out the ruin, you can retrace your steps back to the trailhead, or if you have more

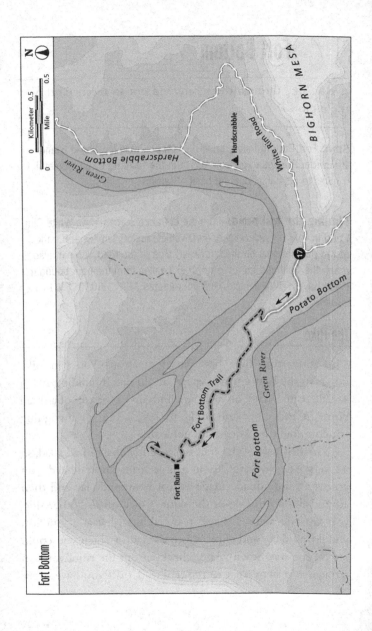

Fort Bottom

time and energy, you can continue on down to the bottom, the site of a historic ranching operation.

If you opt to climb up to the top of the butte, the trail gets a little rough for about 100 yards, including two little cliffs you need to climb, but it's still safe. Once on top, you can see the structure, but don't go in it or touch it. Tower structures are very common throughout the Southwest. This is the only known tower structure within Canyonlands National Park.

The trail down to the bottom is easier, so if you have children, this might be a better choice instead of climbing up to the top of the butte. When you get down there, you can see one old cabin and an area where a recent fire has destroyed some majestic old cottonwoods. The cabin was built in 1895 for people traveling the Green River and for people going to a planned tuberculosis sanitarium at the confluence of the Green and Colorado Rivers, which was never built.

You can also take a pleasant nap on the bank of the Green River.

# 18  Gooseneck

A short walk with a scenic view that serves as a welcome relief from traveling the White Rim Road.

**Start:** Gooseneck turnoff on White Rim Road

**Distance:** 0.6 mile; out-and-back

**Maps:** Trails Illustrated Island in the Sky and USGS Musselman Arch

**Finding the trailhead:** From the entrance station drive 6.4 miles on the White Rim Road and park at the parking area on the left (east) side of the road. GPS coordinates: N27 17.843' / W109 46.433'

## The Hike

At this point on White Rim Road, due east of the Island in the Sky visitor center, you'll have been bumping along on some of the rockiest sections of road, so a little hike might be just what you need. If so, the Gooseneck will be just right. This pleasant trail would be a great diversion from your mountain bike or four-wheeler.

It's less than a half mile one-way. Enjoy a snack, and relax for a few moments at this very scenic overlook.

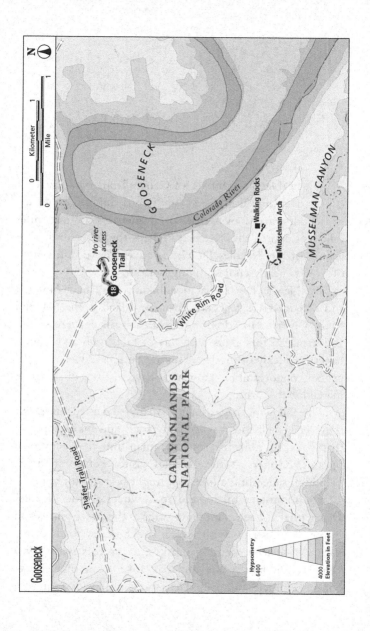

Gooseneck

# Canyonlands National Park: The Needles

The Needles District of Canyonlands National Park is a high desert paradise. It is a jumbled landscape dominated by a series of distinctive sandstone spires called, of course, the Needles. Perhaps the other distinctive feature of the Needles District is an extensive trail system that offers nearly endless hiking options.

The Needles District has more hiking trails (about 74 miles) and a better variety of trails than the Island in the Sky and Maze Districts. In addition, this area is, in general, set up and managed for hikers with lots of loop trails and a good selection of easy or moderate hiking options as well as backpacking opportunities. Most trails have sections of slickrock marked with cairns.

The following pages include many suggested hikes, but the Needles District has so many trails and hiking options that you can easily get out the map and find additional options. Rangers at the Needles visitor center are most helpful in suggesting a hike that might be right for you.

For mountain bikers and four-wheelers, the Needles District has at least as much to offer as the Maze and Island in the Sky Districts with several backcountry roads. Some have well-placed scenic campsites, so visitors with 4WD vehicles can base camp and day hike from their backcountry vehicle camp. In fact, some trailheads require a high-clearance, 4WD vehicle with low-range gearing and an experienced driver to access.

The Needles District has a great visitor center about a quarter mile past the entrance station. The Needles Campground has twenty-six campsites with picnic tables, fire rings (bring your own wood), a water supply (spring through fall), a dishwashing station, and two comfort stations with flush toilets. The campsites go on a first-come/first-served basis, and you'll be lucky to get one during the peak seasons, spring and fall. The Needles District also has three group sites, which can be reserved in advance. Both individual sites in the campground and group sites have nominal fees.

The Needles District also has more surface water than other sections of Canyonlands National Park and Arches National Park. In spring, you can often find flowing streams in several canyons. However, be sure to carry your own water instead of depending on unreliable desert water sources. In spring, the entire area can be awash with wildflowers.

## Fear the Night

The Needles District attracts thousands of hikers, some inexperienced. One fairly common—and serious—problem is that inexperienced hikers underestimate how much time it takes to complete a hike and get caught by nightfall, in many cases without a flashlight or headlamp.

Even with a flashlight or headlamp, following Needles trails at night can be challenging. Most trails have slickrock sections and go along canyon washes, making it easy to miss a cairn and get off the trail. Be extra careful not to underestimate the time a hike will take or overestimate your physical abilities, keeping in mind that summer heat can significantly slow you down.

## Getting to the Needles District

From Moab take US 191 south for 40 miles and turn right (west) onto SR 211. Follow this paved road 35 miles to the Needles District entrance station. Be careful not to take Needles Overlook Road, which takes off a few miles before the correct junction. This road does not take you to Canyonlands National Park. Watch for the Canyonlands National Park sign before turning. From Monticello, drive 14 miles north on US 191 and turn left (west) onto SR 211.

# 19 Roadside Ruin

A very short walk and good opportunity to learn about local plant life and cultural history.

**Start:** Roadside Ruin Parking Area

**Distance:** 0.3 mile; loop

**Maps:** Trails Illustrated Needles and USGS The Loop

**Finding the trailhead:** Drive 0.6 mile from the Needles entrance station and park on the south side of the road in the well-signed Roadside Ruin Parking Area. GPS coordinates: N9 47.091' / W109 45.750'

## The Hike

This hike offers an easy introduction to the Canyonlands and its cultural history and plant life. At the trailhead, for a token fee, you can get a brochure for this self-guided interpretive trail.

Along the short, flat route, signs identify key native plant species, and the brochure describes these plants and how American Indians used them. Halfway around the loop, you can see a granary typical of the ancient Puebloan structures found throughout the park, although few are as well-preserved as this one.

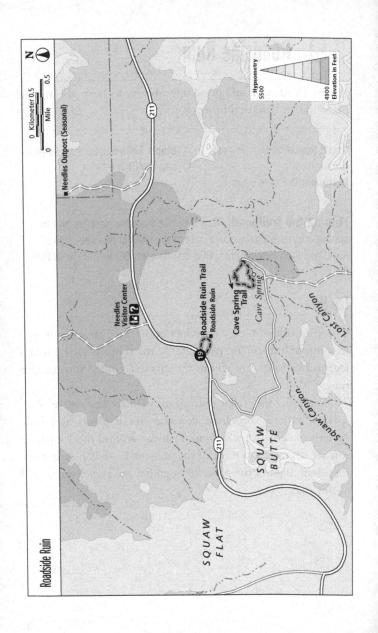

Roadside Ruin

# 20 Cave Spring

An opportunity to learn about the cultural history and desert plant life on a short hike.

**Start:** Cave Spring Parking Area
**Distance:** 0.6 mile; loop

**Maps:** Trails Illustrated Needles and USGS The Loop

**Finding the trailhead:** Drive 0.9 mile west from the Needles entrance station, take a left (south) onto a paved road (sign points to Salt Creek), and go 0.5 mile before taking another left (east) onto a dirt road. The unpaved road ends in 1.2 miles at the parking area and trailhead for the Cave Spring Trail. GPS coordinates: N9 26.129' / W109 45.083'

## The Hike

If you're in the Needles area and have an extra hour, the Cave Spring hike is a pleasant way to spend it. The trailhead is conveniently located, and this short hike offers lots of diversity. At the trailhead, for a token fee, you can pick up a brochure that explains the area's history and plant life.

The small loop trail goes by ruins of historic ranching operations that were active here until 1975, when livestock grazing was abandoned in Canyonlands National Park. Please honor the barriers put up by the NPS to preserve this part of the area's history. Later, the trail goes by Cave Spring and then passes by some rock art left by the Ancestral Puebloans who inhabited the area a thousand years ago. Please don't touch these art treasures.

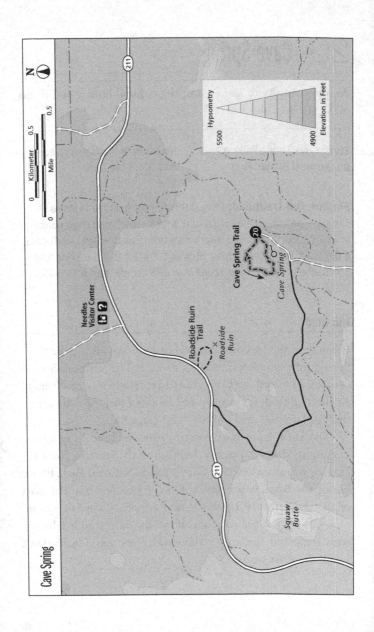

Cave Spring

After you finish enjoying the signs of both recent and ancient history, hike around a large "Canyonlands mushroom" and climb a safety ladder to a slickrock flat. Here you get the experience of following cairns over slickrock and also get a great view of many of the area's main features, such as the Needles, North Six-shooter Peak, and South Six-shooter Peak.

Interpretive signs along the trail identify many of the high desert's most common plant species.

# 21 Pothole Point

A short hike to learn about life in desert potholes.

**Start:** Pothole Point Parking Area
**Distance:** 0.6 mile; loop

**Maps:** Trails Illustrated Needles and USGS The Loop

**Finding the trailhead:** From the Needles entrance station, drive 5.1 miles and park on the left (west) side of the road in the Pothole Point Parking Area. GPS coordinates: N10 13.371' / W109 48.367'

## The Hike

If you need a little exercise or want to take small children for an easy, safe hike where they might learn something about desert ecology, Pothole Point is an excellent choice. At the trailhead, for a token fee, you can buy a small brochure explaining the fascinating ecology of potholes.

Most of this hike follows a string of cairns over slickrock. The name Pothole Point comes from the numerous "potholes" that have formed in the slickrock along the trail. The potholes trap water after a desert rain. The rainwater is mildly acidic and ever so slowly enlarges the pothole. An intricate, symbiotic animal community featuring shrimp, worms, snails, and perhaps even a Great Basin spadefoot toad gradually develops in some potholes. If you're lucky enough to visit Pothole Point shortly after a rain, you can observe these tiny ecosystems.

Over time, the wind continuously blows dirt, sand, and small bits of organic material into the potholes. Eventually plants take root in the thin layer of soil. The first sign of life

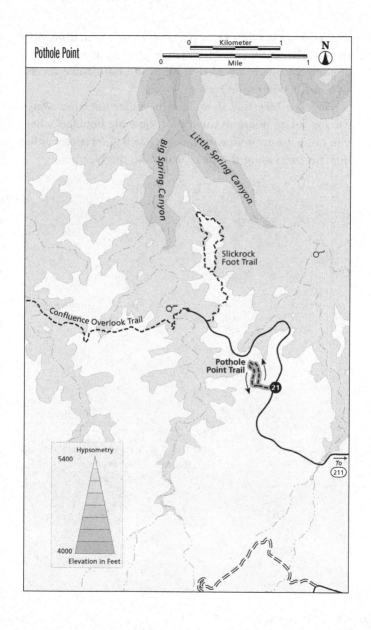

in a pothole is often the cryptobiotic soil, which provides the foundation for growth of larger plants. The end result is a "pothole garden," a pocket of miniature, bonsai-like vegetation in a bowl of solid rock.

You can hike this short loop in either direction. Watch for a spur trail going to the top of some big boulders where you can get a great view of the surrounding terrain in either direction, including the area's namesake, the Needles.

# 22 Slickrock Foot Trail

A scenic trip through the geology of the Canyonlands.

**Start:** Slickrock Foot Trail Parking Area

**Distance:** 2.4 miles; lollipop loop

**Maps:** Trails Illustrated Needles and USGS The Loop

**Finding the trailhead:** From the Needles entrance station, drive 6.4 miles and park on the right (north) side of the road at the Slickrock Foot Trail Parking Area, just before the end of the road. GPS coordinates: N10 37.428' / W109 48.867'

## The Hike

Either a beginner or experienced hiker with a half day to spend in the Needles District will enjoy spending it on the Slickrock Foot Trail. Many hikes in the Needles follow canyon bottoms, but this trail stays high and gives an overall perspective of the entire southeastern corner of Canyonlands National Park.

The NPS suggests this trail to inexperienced hikers so they can take a look at the entire area before deciding on their next hike. On this trail, beginners also learn how to follow cairns and hike on slickrock. For the beginner who has only walked well-defined dirt trails, this hike might be a little adventurous, but it certainly isn't dangerous. The trail is easy to follow, with lots of cairns marking the way. Well-placed signs mark the way to four viewpoints and the point where the lollipop loop begins.

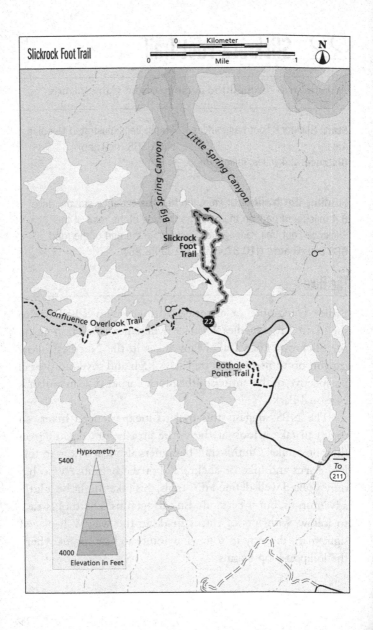

At the trailhead, for a token fee, pick up a brochure written for this hike. It describes much of the geology of the area and is keyed specifically to the four viewpoints along the trail.

Take the hike counterclockwise as indicated by an NPS sign about a half mile up the trail where the loop section of the trail begins, which is just after the first viewpoint where you get a panoramic view of the entire region and many of the major landmarks—Six-shooter Peak, Elaterite Butte, Cathedral Butte, the La Sal Mountains, Ekker Butte, and, of course, the Needles.

The trail stays on the ridge between Little Spring and Big Spring Canyons. At the second viewpoint, you can get a good view into the upper reaches of Little Spring Canyon.

After the third viewpoint, the trail turns west and then south. You can take a long look at the region's namesake, the Needles, as you walk along.

At the last viewpoint, you can look down into the massive Big Spring Canyon. In spring, you might see a stream flowing in the distance far below. The brochure gives you a great geology lesson from this viewpoint, so plan on spending extra time here to identify all the different strata that make up the canyon's awesome cliffs.

After you leave the fourth viewpoint, it's another mile or so back to the trailhead, most of the trail following the east flank of Big Spring Canyon.

# 23  Castle Arch

A short, uphill walk to a big arch accessed by a 4WD road.

**Start:** Castle Arch Trailhead near the end of Horse Canyon Road

**Distance:** 0.8 mile; out-and-back

**Maps:** Trails Illustrated Needles and USGS South Six-shooter Peak

**Finding the trailhead:** From the entrance station, drive 0.9 mile and turn left (south) onto a paved road (marked Salt Creek). Follow this road for 0.5 mile and then turn left (east) onto a gravel road. Follow this road for 0.8 mile until you see the sign for Salt Creek. Turn right (south) here and go about a quarter mile to the gate at the entrance to Salt Creek Road. Day-use and overnight camping permits are required. Get them at the visitor center. Use the combination on your permit to open the gate and follow Salt Creek Road and then Horse Canyon Road to the trailhead at the end of Horse Canyon Road. GPS coordinates: N3 47.486' / W109 43.867'

## The Hike

Just before the end of Horse Canyon Road is the trailhead sign for Castle Arch Trail and a spot to pull off the main road. From here, the trail heads west through a heavily vegetated valley on a slightly uphill grade, nicely carpeted with oak leaves but a bit primitive and brushy in places. It is a real treat for students of high desert vegetation. You can see the arch throughout most of the hike. However, the trail doesn't go to the arch and in fact has no clearly definable end. Instead, it just gets more and more faint, and you'll know when it's time to take one last look at the arch and head back to your vehicle.

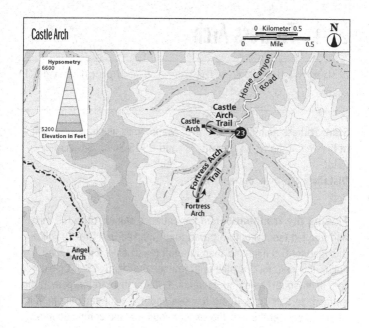

If you're interested in more exercise after you get back to your vehicle, you can walk instead of drive about a quarter mile down the road to the Fortress Arch Trailhead.

# 24 Fortress Arch

A short wash walk to a massive arch at the end of a 4WD road.

**Start:** Fortress Arch Trailhead at the end of the Horse Canyon Road
**Distance:** 0.6 mile; out-and-back

**Maps:** Trails Illustrated Needles and USGS South Six-shooter Peak

**Finding the trailhead:** From the entrance station, drive 0.9 mile and turn left (south) onto a paved road (marked Salt Creek). Follow this road for 0.5 mile and then turn left (east) onto a gravel road. Follow this road for 0.8 mile until you see the sign for Salt Creek. Turn right (south) here and go about a quarter mile to the gate at the entrance to Salt Creek Road. Day-use and overnight camping permits are required. Get them at the visitor center Use the combination on your permit to open the gate and follow Salt Creek Road and then Horse Canyon Road to the trailhead at the end of Horse Canyon Road. GPS coordinates: N3 47.486' / W109 43.867'

## The Hike

The Fortress Arch Trail starts right at the end of Horse Canyon Road. From the parking area, it heads up a dry wash and stays there, with easy walking all the way. The trail ends near a big, flat rock that makes an excellent spot to relax for a few minutes while you marvel at this massive arch.

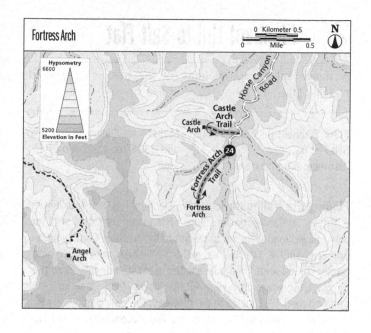

# 25  Elephant Hill to Salt Flat

A shuttle hike through some of the best scenery in the Needles District.

**Start:** Elephant Hill Trailhead or Salt Flat Trailhead
**Distance:** 4.9 miles; shuttle

**Maps:** Trails Illustrated Needles and USGS The Loop and Druid Arch

**Finding the trailhead:** To find the Elephant Hill Trailhead, drive 3.1 miles from the entrance station on the main park road until you see a paved road going off to the left to the Needles Campground and Elephant Hill. Take this left and 0.3 mile later, take a right onto another paved road. Then take another right 0.5 mile later onto the unpaved, two-wheel-drive Elephant Hill Access Road. Once on the unpaved road, it's 3 miles to the trailhead. Drive slowly on this road, especially around several blind corners. GPS coordinates: N8 30.272' / W109 49.617'

To leave a second car or be picked up at the Salt Flat Trailhead, drive about 2.7 miles west from the Needles entrance station and turn left into the Needles Campground. After entering the campground area, the road forks. Both forks go to trailheads with access to the same trails. However, the left-hand fork takes you to the trailhead with the shortest access route to the backcountry. The right-hand fork and its respective trailhead are used mostly by campers staying in the campground. GPS coordinates: N8 36.487' / W109 48.217'

## The Hike

If your party has two vehicles, or you're staying at the Needles Campground and one member of your party volunteers to drop you off at Elephant Hill Trailhead, this is a great day

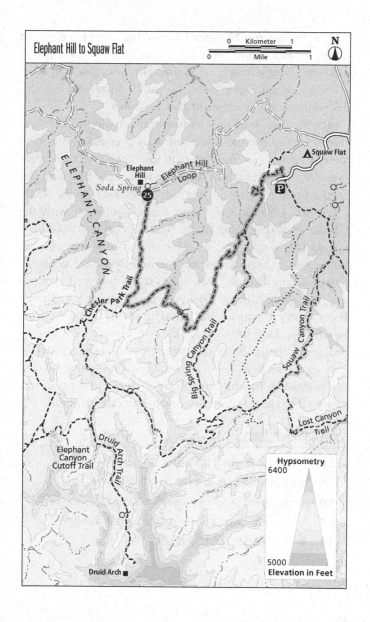

hike. Although the Needles District has a great variety of quality hiking opportunities, there aren't many hikes in the moderate, 5-mile range, so if that suits you, this trail is an excellent choice. You can do the shuttle in reverse, but this description starts at Elephant Hill Trailhead.

Right after leaving Elephant Hill Trailhead, the trail climbs a steep but short hill and then goes through a small joint between two rock formations. Then the trail heads over a fairly flat stretch of slickrock with a good view of Big Spring Canyon off to the east and the Needles to the south.

At the 1.5-mile mark, you reach a junction with the Chesler Park Trail going to the right. Go left (east) and head toward Big Spring Canyon. This stretch of trail is pleasant walking as it alternates between a well-defined, packed dirt trail and short slickrock sections. At the 4-mile mark, you see the Big Spring Canyon Trail coming in from the right and Backcountry Campsite BS1 straight ahead. If you want an easy backpacking trip, you could try to reserve this campsite and spend the night in the desert before covering the last mile or so back to Salt Flat Trailhead or Campground. If you're heading for the campground, watch for a cutoff trail going off to the left just before you reach the trailhead.

## Miles and Directions

**0.0** Start at the Elephant Hill Trailhead.

**1.5** Junction with trail to Salt Flat Trailhead; turn left.

**4.0** Junction with Big Spring Canyon Trail; turn left.

**4.4** Junction with the campground's Loop B trail; turn right.

**4.9** Arrive at the Salt Flat Trailhead.

# 26 The Joint Trail

Perhaps the most famous day hike in the Needles, but one of the most difficult to access.

**Start:** Chesler Park / Joint Trailhead

**Distance:** 2 miles; out-and-back

**Maps:** Trails Illustrated Needles and USGS Druid Arch

**Finding the trailhead:** You have two options for reaching this trailhead, but both require a high-clearance, 4WD vehicle with low-range gearing and the skill and experience to drive it.

The shortest but perhaps most challenging route (5 miles) leaves from the Elephant Hill Trailhead. To find the Elephant Hill Trailhead, drive 3.1 miles from the entrance station on the main park road until you see a paved road going off to the left to the Needles Campground and Elephant Hill. Take this left and 0.3 mile later, take a right onto another paved road. Then take another right 0.5 mile later onto the unpaved, two-wheel-drive Elephant Hill Access Road. Once on the unpaved road, it's 3 miles to the trailhead. Drive slowly on this road, especially around several blind corners. GPS coordinates: N8 30.272' / W109 49.617'

From the trailhead, start driving up the Elephant Hill backcountry road, which will challenge any 4WD enthusiast. After 1.5 miles, turn left (south) onto the one-way road to Devils Kitchen. Go 0.5 mile past the spur road to Devils Kitchen camp and turn left (south) again and go 3.5 miles until you turn left (east) one more time and go another 0.5 to the Joint Trailhead.

The longer and nearly as challenging route starts from the Needles entrance station. Drive east out of the park on SR 211 for 13.7 miles and turn right (south) onto a gravel road marked Elk Mountain and Beef Basin. If you're coming from the east, the turnoff is 20 miles from US 191. Follow this unpaved road, which gets gradually worse, for 43 miles until you see the park boundary. From here, drive 4.7 miles into the park until you see the junction with the road to Chesler Park Trailhead. Turn right (east) here and go 0.5 mile until the road dead-ends at the trailhead. The trailhead has a vault toilet and picnic tables. GPS coordinates: N6 12.854' / W109 51.983'

## The Hike

The Joint Trail is an excellent choice for those who want a little adventure (but not danger) as long as somebody has the skill to drive very gnarly roads with a high-clearance, 4WD vehicle. In fact, getting to this trailhead is the hardest and most adventurous part of this trip. This route goes through some very interesting terrain, but it is not long or strenuous.

The hike starts out uphill on a moderately rugged, rocky trail with cairns showing the way. In about a half mile, it dips into a long, narrow joint between two rock formations. From here, it's like hiking in a narrow slot canyon for about a quarter mile. A few spots require a handhold to scramble over rocks in the Joint, and near the end, you climb man-made but rustic "stairs" just before you finally emerge from the depths of the Joint.

Just as you break out into daylight, you see a sign indicating a short viewpoint trail heading right (south) from the junction. The Chesler Park Trail veers off to the left (east). The viewpoint is only about a quarter mile from the sign, but it involves a short climb onto a slickrock ledge. This might be a little nerve-racking for parents hiking with children, but it's fairly safe. The steepest spots are made easier with little steps chipped out of the solid rock. At the viewpoint, you get a fantastic view of Chesler Park—it's the perimeter of stately, multihued sandstone formations including the Pinnacle to the north. After soaking in the view and having a pleasant

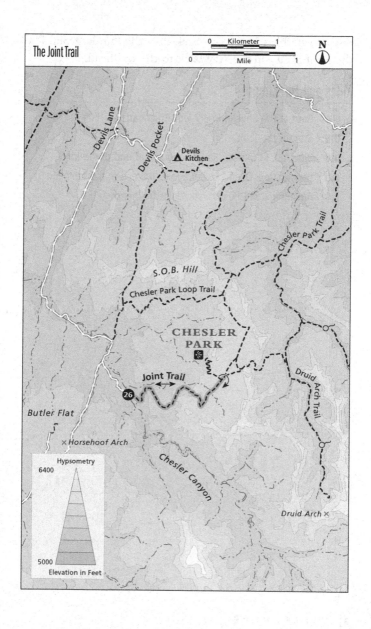

The Joint Trail

Kilometer

Mile

N

Devils Lane

Devils Pocket

Devils Kitchen ▲

Chesler Park Trail

S.O.B. Hill

Chesler Park Loop Trail

CHESLER PARK

Joint Trail

26

Druid Arch Trail

Butler Flat

× Horsehoof Arch

Chesler Canyon

Druid Arch ×

Hypsometry

6400

5000

Elevation in Feet

rest and perhaps lunch, it's back into the "underground" of the Joint again on the way back to the trailhead.

## Miles and Directions

**0.0**   Start at the Chesler Park / Joint Trailhead.

**0.5**   Start of the Joint.

**0.8**   Side trail to Chesler Park Overlook and end of the Joint.

**1.0**   Chesler Park Overlook. Retrace your steps to the trailhead.

**2.0**   Arrive back at Chesler Park / Joint Trailhead.

# 27 Chesler Park Loop

A popular, extra–scenic loop hike.

**Start:** Chesler Park / Joint Trail trailhead
**Distance:** 5.0 miles; loop

**Maps:** Trails Illustrated Needles and USGS Druid Arch

**Finding the trailhead:** You have two options for reaching this trailhead, but both require a high-clearance, 4WD vehicle with low-range gearing and the skill and experience to drive it.

The shortest but perhaps more challenging route (5 miles) leaves from the Elephant Hill Trailhead. To find the Elephant Hill Trailhead, drive 3.1 miles from the entrance station on the main park road until you see a paved road going off to the left to the Needles Campground and Elephant Hill. Take this left and 0.3 mile later, take a right onto another paved road. Then take another right 0.5 mile later onto the unpaved, two-wheel-drive Elephant Hill Access Road. Once on the unpaved road, it's 3 miles to the trailhead. Drive slowly on this road, especially around several blind corners. GPS coordinates: N8 30.272' / W109 49.617'

At the trailhead, start up the Elephant Hill backcountry road, which will challenge any 4WD enthusiast. After 1.5 miles, turn left (south) onto the one-way road to Devils Kitchen. Go 0.5 mile past the spur road to Devils Kitchen camp and turn left (south) again and go 3.5 miles until you turn left (east) one more time and go another 0.5 mile to the Joint Trailhead.

The longer and nearly as challenging route starts from the Needles entrance station. Drive east out of the park on SR 211 for 13.7 miles and turn right (south) onto a gravel road marked ELK MOUNTAIN AND BEEF BASIN. If you're coming from the east, the turnoff is 20 miles from US 191. Follow this unpaved road, which gets gradually worse, for 43 miles until you see the park boundary. From here, drive 4.7 miles into the park until you see the junction with the road to Chesler Park Trailhead. Turn right (east) here and go 0.5 mile until the road dead-ends at the trailhead. The trailhead has a vault toilet and picnic tables. GPS coordinates: N6 12.854' / W109 51.983'

## The Hike

If you like to save the best until last, take this trail clockwise. This involves walking on a road for the first mile, but it's easy going, and you're unlikely to see any vehicles.

The road forks 0.5 mile after leaving the trailhead, with the left fork going off to Beef Basin. Take a right and walk another 0.4 mile until you see a sign for the Devils Pocket. The sign for this trail is not right along the road, so watch for it a few feet up the trail.

The next section of trail involves a gradual climb up to a junction with the trail through the Pinnacle to Devils Kitchen Camp. You go right (east) at this junction and head for Chesler Park.

You go through one rocky section with one short, steep pitch before coming out into the gorgeous Chesler Park, a huge grassy flatland ringed by colorful sandstone spires. The trail goes along the north edge of the park for less than a half mile before hitting the next junction.

At this junction, turn right (south) and toward the Joint Trail. Follow the east edge of Chesler Park on a nicely defined and packed dirt trail for 1.3 miles to the next junction. Just less than halfway through this section, you see Backcountry Campsite CP1 on your left. It's back from the trail about 100 yards, out of sight among several large boulders. This is a great choice if you're staying overnight. It's shady and more private than the four campsites farther down the trail.

When you reach the junction with the Elephant Canyon Cutoff Trail (which goes off to the east), go straight. In less than 50 feet, you see a side trail to Backcountry Campsites CP3, CP4, and CP5 off to your right and, a few steps down the trail, CP2 off to your left. CP2 and CP3 are fairly close to the trail; CP3 has the best view of Chesler Park. CP4 and CP5 are farther away from the main trail and more private. All the campsites are tucked amid gigantic boulders where you can always find shade. You also see some signs of historic ranching operations, which operated in Chesler Park before the national park was created.

From the campsites, the trail is flat and easy walking. Long ago, parts of this trail were a primitive road. In about a half mile, you reach the start of the Joint and the side trail going to the left to the Chesler Park Overlook. Even though you've been walking through or on the edge of Chesler Park for a long time, you want to check out this viewpoint. It gives you a grand vista you don't get from the lower-elevation trails. The viewpoint is only about a quarter mile off the main trail and well worth the little climb up to a slickrock platform where you get a better-than-postcard panoramic vista of Chesler Park and the sandstone formations surrounding it.

Back at the viewpoint sign, the trail dives into the Joint, a large crack between rock formations. As you climb down man-made rock stairs to get to its depths, you might think you're not really on a trail, but you are. You stay in the Joint for another quarter mile or so. It's a tight squeeze in spots, but you shouldn't have any problems unless you're built like an NFL offensive lineman. However, you might have to push and twist to get a big backpack through the Joint. Logs placed in strategic points help you get down short drops.

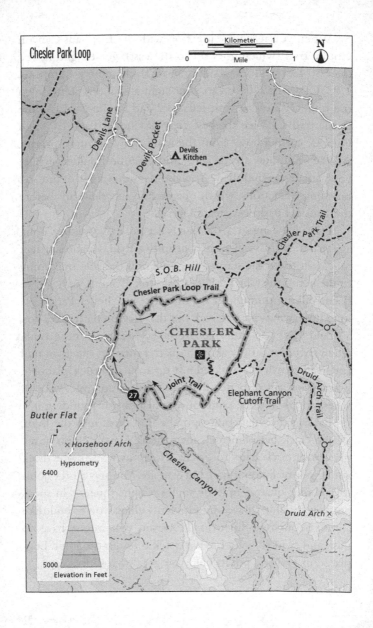

Chesler Park Loop

After you come out into sunlight again, it's about a half mile on a fairly rocky trail down to the Chesler Park / Joint Trailhead, where you started the loop hike.

## Miles and Directions

**0.0** Start at Chesler Park / Joint Trailhead.

**0.5** Beef Basin Road junction.

**0.9** Devils Pocket Trailhead.

**1.3** Junction with Chesler Park Cutoff Trail; turn right.

**2.6** Junction with Chesler Park Trail; turn right.

**3.0** Backcountry Campsite CP1.

**3.4** Junction with Elephant Canyon Cutoff Trail.

**3.5** Junction with the Joint Trail; turn right.

**3.6** Backcountry Campsites CP2, CP3, CP4, and CP5.

**4.2** Chesler Park Overlook and start of the Joint.

**4.8** End of the Joint.

**5.0** Arrive back at Chesler Park / Joint Trailhead.

# 28 Devils Pocket Loop

A great day hike for hikers with a 4WD vehicle to reach the trailhead.

**Start:** Devils Kitchen Trailhead
**Distance:** 5.1 miles; loop

**Maps:** Trails Illustrated Needles and USGS The Loop and Druid Arch

**Finding the trailhead:** You have two options for reaching this trailhead, but both require a high-clearance, 4WD vehicle with low-range gearing and the skill and experience to drive it.

The shortest but perhaps more challenging route (5 miles) leaves from the Elephant Hill Trailhead. To find the Elephant Hill Trailhead, drive 3.1 miles from the entrance station on the main park road until you see a paved road going off to the left to the Needles Campground and Elephant Hill. Take this left and 0.3 mile later, take a right onto another paved road. Then take another right 0.5 mile later onto the unpaved, two-wheel-drive Elephant Hill Access Road. Once on the unpaved road, it's 3 miles to the trailhead. Drive slowly on this road, especially around several blind corners. GPS coordinates: N8 30.272' / W109 49.617'

From the Elephant Hill Trailhead, start driving up the Elephant Hill backcountry road. The first 1.5-mile stretch of this road goes over Elephant Hill, technical four-wheel-driving most of the way. At the 1.5-mile mark, turn left (south) onto one-way road to Devils Kitchen. After 2 miles, turn left (east) onto the Devils Kitchen mile-long spur road to the Devils Kitchen Camp and Trailhead.

The longer, but still difficult, option starts from the Needles entrance station. Drive east out of the park on SR 211 for 13.7 miles and turn right (south) onto a gravel road marked Elk Mountain and Beef Basin. If you're coming from the east, the turnoff is 20 miles from US 191. Follow this unpaved road, which gets gradually worse, for 43 miles until you see the park boundary.

From the south boundary, drive north up Devils Lane Road for 4.7 miles to the junction with the Chesler Park Trailhead road. Continue straight (north) through the junction for another 3.1 miles, going over the infamous S.O.B. Hill until you see a junction with Devils Kitchen Road. Turn right (east) here and go another mile to Devils Kitchen Camp and Trailhead, where you find four premier vehicle campsites, a vault toilet, and picnic tables. GPS coordinates: N8 15.019' / W109 51.683'

## The Hike

If you're camped at Devils Kitchen, this is an excellent choice for a day hike. The loop can be taken from either direction, but the clockwise route is described here.

The trail starts just to the left of the sign at the south end of the campground and heads along a canyon wash for a few hundred yards. It then starts a gradual climb up toward the Pinnacle, a majestic sandstone formation and the highlight of this section of the Canyonlands. The trail alternates between slickrock and well-defined dirt trail for the entire 2.5 miles to the junction with the Chesler Park Trail.

Take a right (southwest) at this junction. You quickly start a fairly serious but short climb to a narrow "pass" in the Pinnacle. At the top of the pass, pause to look both ways for incredible views of Elephant Canyon (to the northeast) and Chesler Park (to the southwest). It's a very short section of trail, only 0.2 mile to the junction just downhill from the pass on the edge of Chesler Park. If you want to make this an overnighter, you should try to reserve Backcountry Campsite CP1, which is 0.6 mile south of this junction. The overnighter option adds about 1.2 miles to your trip.

From this junction, take a right (west) and walk on a packed dirt path along the north perimeter of Chesler

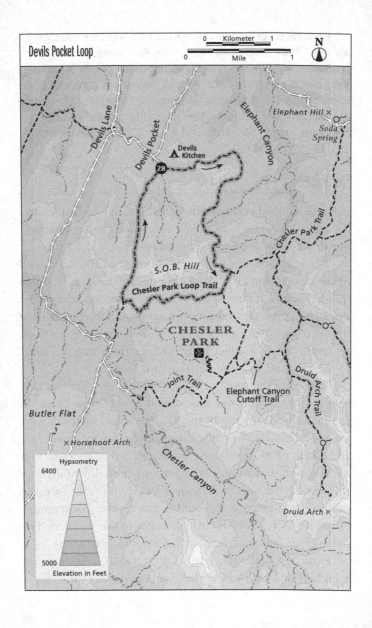

## Devils Pocket Loop

Kilometer
0 — 1
Mile
0 — 1

N

Devils Lane

Devils Pocket

Devils Kitchen

28

Elephant Canyon

Elephant Hill ×

Soda Spring

Chesler Park Trail

S.O.B. Hill

Chesler Park Loop Trail

**CHESLER PARK**

Joint Trail

Elephant Canyon Cutoff Trail

Druid Arch Trail

Butler Flat

× Horsehoof Arch

Chesler Canyon

Druid Arch ×

Hypsometry

6400

5000

Elevation in Feet

Park for about a half mile before heading down a rocky section toward the next junction. Here take another right (north) and start climbing up to the second pass through the Pinnacle.

After descending from the pass, the trail goes through a series of open parks, mostly on packed dirt with a few stretches of loose sand. Less than a half mile from Devils Kitchen, you'll see Backcountry Campsite DP1 on your right. This is an adorable site about 100 yards off the trail and nestled between two big boulders under some piñon pines. The rest of the trail is flat on loose sand until you come back to Devils Kitchen right by the sign where you started.

## Miles and Directions

**0.0** Start at Devils Kitchen Trailhead.

**2.3** Junction with trail to Elephant Hill Trailhead; turn right.

**2.6** Junction with Chesler Park Trail; turn right.

**3.7** Junction with Devils Pocket Trail; turn right.

**4.8** Backcountry Campsite DP1.

**5.1** Arrive back at Devils Kitchen Camp and Trailhead.

# Canyonlands National Park: The Maze, Orange Cliffs, and Horseshoe Canyon

When people use the old adage "in the middle of nowhere," they could easily be talking about the Maze, and it would be a compliment.

Most people have never been to a place as remote as the Maze, and getting there can be a great warm-up for experiencing this remote district of Canyonlands National Park. Whether you come from Hite, Hanksville, or Green River, you definitely get the feeling of being out of touch with civilization long before you reach the park boundary. Then, once you start slowly maneuvering your vehicle along the primitive roads into the Maze, you realize how vital it is to be totally self-reliant. Very few national parks can come close the extreme remoteness of the Maze.

Self-reliance is the cornerstone of the management policy of the Maze District. This network of twisted sandstone canyons is for rugged individuals who can take care of themselves and their vehicle. There's no gas station, restaurant, or room service for 50-plus miles in any direction. And even those 50 miles don't tell the true story because it might take half a day to cover that distance on these roads.

In many national parks, including other districts of Canyonlands, the NPS has big visitor centers with bookstores, backcountry offices and multiple rangers to help hikers find the best routes for them. The Maze, however, only has a remote ranger station with limited staffing. The rangers there are at least as helpful as anywhere else, but everything is smaller and limited, including the number of visitors, compared to other districts in Canyonlands or Arches. The Maze District of Canyonlands National Park combined with the Orange Cliffs Unit of Glen Canyon National Recreation Area (NRA) is larger than many national parks, but once you leave the Hans Flat Ranger Station, there are no services—no guided tours, no facilities, no toilets, not even an entrance station. You're on your own, so prepare for it.

In the Maze District, you should measure roads and trails in hours instead of miles. A 1-mile trail can take an hour to hike; a 5-mile stretch of road can take 2 or 3 hours to drive. Under any circumstances, don't be in a hurry.

After a heavy rain, the clay coating on some roads in the Maze (particularly the Flint Trail) makes them too slippery to drive. Also, in winter months, ice and snow can make the roads impassable. During winter, the Flint Trail is usually closed.

Before you go to the Maze District, make sure you know where you're going, what to bring, and how to prepare. This isn't like going to other national parks. If you show up without the necessary gear to survive on your own, you won't enjoy the Maze District. Yet it happens all the time. People show up in a rented SUV that's not supposed to be driven off paved roads, and they expect to get into the Maze. A very bad idea!

Glen Canyon, including the Orange Cliffs Special Management Unit, has started charging an entrance fee. The fee is not currently required in the Orange Cliffs if you have a camping permit but is required for day use in the Orange Cliffs.

## Getting to Hans Flat Ranger Station

From Hanksville, go north 21 miles on SR 24 and turn right (east) onto a major unpaved, two-wheel-drive road marked with signs for the Glen Canyon NRA and Canyonlands National Park. From here, it's 46 miles to Hans Flat Ranger Station, with a right-hand turn at the 24-mile mark; both junctions are well-signed.

From Hite, take SR 95 north for 2 miles and turn right (east) onto an unpaved, high-clearance, two-wheel-drive road. After 32 miles, this road turns into a high-clearance, 4WD road, which includes ascending the Flint Trail (which weather conditions can make impassable) to reach Hans Flat. It's about 59 miles to the Hans Flat Ranger Station, with several junctions once you get to the park, all well-signed. It takes most drivers 5–6 hours to drive from SR 95 to Hans Flat, depending on road conditions. Unless you have a camping reservation, you will need to pay an entrance fee at the Hite Ranger Station.

If you're coming from Green River, go to the middle of town and watch for Long Street. Turn south onto Long Street and follow it to the edge of town, following the signs to the airport. Be sure to take a gradual left turn onto an unpaved road 2 miles after passing under I-70 and stay on it for 68 miles to Hans Flat Ranger Station. At the 28-mile mark, take a left at the junction with Dugout Spring Road, and at the 46-mile mark, take another left at the Hanksville junction. This road is usually passable with a high-clearance, two-wheel-drive vehicle, but at times deep sand areas can require 4WD capability. To be safe, bring a high-clearance, 4WD vehicle. You'll need it to go into the Maze anyway.

If you want to see Horseshoe Canyon (and you'll be missing something if you don't), watch for a small sign at the 41-mile mark that says HORSESHOE CANYON FOOT TRAIL 2 MILES. If you hit the junction with the road from Hanksville, you've gone about 5 miles too far. If you're coming from Hanksville, take a left at the same junction and go 5 miles north.

You can call the Hans Flat Ranger Station (435-259-2652) for help, but only during regular office hours (8 a.m. to 5 p.m.). Do not call from 5 p.m. to 8 a.m. unless it's an emergency.

## Special Regulations

In addition to park regulations, the NPS has a few special rules for the Maze, Orange Cliffs, and Horseshoe Canyon sections of the park.

- No wood fires are allowed, either in the vehicle campsites or while backpacking.

- Vehicle campers can have charcoal fires, but they must use a fire pan and remove the ashes along with other garbage. Pans can be purchased at the Hans Flat Ranger Station.

- Anybody using the vehicle campsites in the Maze District or Orange Cliffs Unit of Glen Canyon NRA must have and use a portable toilet and remove human waste along with all other garbage. An ammo can or plastic bag can be used, provided the bags are specialty human waste carryout bags such as the Wag Bag or Rest Stop Two Bag. Portable toilets can be purchased at the Hans Flat Ranger Station.

- Backpackers can bury their human waste, but they must carry out their toilet paper.
- Backpack camping is at-large, but there are limits set for each backcountry zone. You don't need to get your backpacking permit until you get to Hans Flat, but you'd be wise to call in advance for a reservation. Don't make the effort to get there and then find out that you can't go backpacking because your chosen zone is full.
- Backpacking group size limit is five people.
- Vehicle permits have a limit of nine people and three vehicles, with the exception of Flint Seep, where up to sixteen people can camp.
- In Horseshoe Canyon, groups larger than twenty people must be accompanied by a ranger. To arrange for a guided tour, call the Hans Flat Ranger Station between 8 a.m. and 4:30 p.m. at (435) 259-2652, but only between 8 a.m. and 5 p.m.
- Pets are not allowed (even in your vehicle) in the Maze District, Horseshoe Canyon, or Orange Cliffs Special Management Unit.
- Off-trail hiking in the Doll House area is prohibited.
- ATVs are not allowed in Canyonlands National Park and Glen Canyon NRA.

## What Kind of Vehicle to Bring to the Maze

Unless you wish to hike great distances to fully experience the Maze District, you must have a high-clearance, 4WD vehicle with low-range gearing. You can see small parts of the Maze with a high-clearance, two-wheel-drive vehicle, but to see the best parts, you'll have to park it and hike long distances. A vehicle with a short wheelbase is best, but even with a long wheelbase, you can usually get through tight corners by backing up once or twice.

The roads in the Maze can deteriorate rapidly when it rains and become treacherous regardless of what kind of vehicle you have. At the same time, fortunately, they dry out relatively fast. If you get caught in a big rain, simply wait a few hours for the roads to dry.

## Call in Advance

The staff at the Hans Flat Ranger Station is trained to help you and eager to answer your questions on the phone. That's much better for both you and the NPS because it's much more difficult to deal with lack of preparation once you're already there. Call in advance between 8 a.m. and 4:30 p.m. at (435) 259-2652. If for some reason you can't get through on the Hans Flat phone system, call the park headquarters at (435) 259-7164. For reservations for vehicle campsites in the Maze, call the park reservation office at (435) 259-4351.

# 29  The Great Gallery

Definitely one of the premier day hikes (closed to camping) in Canyonlands National Park, especially for hikers interested in ancient rock art.

**Start:** West Rim Trailhead
**Distance:** 7 miles; out-and-back

**Maps:** Trails Illustrated Canyon-lands National Park and USGS Sugarloaf Butte

**Finding the trailhead:** There are two ways to get to Horseshoe Canyon. You can take the hike down from the west rim (as described here) or hike into the canyon from the east. To get to the West Rim Trailhead, go 5 miles north of the junction between the Hanksville and Green River access roads to the Maze and watch for a small sign on the east side of the road that says HORSESHOE CANYON FOOT TRAIL 2 MILES. From here, drive 2 miles to the trailhead. GPS coordinates: N28 25.601' / W110 11.983'

## The Hike

Although officially a "detached unit" of Canyonlands National Park, the Horseshoe Canyon area could be better described as a little hidden jewel lost in the desert. When you're driving toward it, you can't see it ahead and you might start to wonder if it's really out there. Then, suddenly, it drops out of the desert right in front of you.

Horseshoe Canyon is definitely worth the time it takes to get there. If you already plan on a few days in the Maze, you won't be disappointed if you spend one day of your vacation enjoying Horseshoe Canyon. If you're going to the Maze from Green River, Horseshoe Canyon is a convenient stop.

The Great Gallery is one of four major rock art sites in Horseshoe Canyon, but the fabulous rock art is only part—and perhaps not the best part—of hiking this remote canyon. Horseshoe Canyon would be well worth the stop without seeing any rock art. It's a fantastic day hike through a secluded canyon lined with majestic cottonwoods and shaded by sheer sandstone cliffs.

Horseshoe Canyon has one other unusual trait. It's one of the few places in the Canyonlands with a fairly reliable water supply that's devoid of the evil tamarisk. NPS staff removed all tamarisk shrubs years ago, and now cottonwoods and other native vegetation have reclaimed the scenic canyon.

Rangers lead hikes into the canyon from the West Rim Trailhead at 9 a.m. on Sat and Sun during the spring and fall. Call the Hans Flat Ranger Station between 8 a.m. and 4:30 p.m. at (435) 259-2652 to verify the schedule. You can also request a guided tour during the week, but there is no guarantee that the NPS, with limited staff and funds, will be able to accommodate your party. If you have a group of twenty or more, you're required to have a ranger along.

You don't have to go with the ranger of course, but it's the best way to get a more complete story and history of Horseshoe Canyon. The ranger stops at each of the four rock art sites to explain the history and prehistory and also comments on the natural history of the hidden canyon along the way. If you want to get good photographs of the rock art panels at the Great Gallery, early afternoon light is usually best.

The hike starts out on and follows an old road from the west rim to the canyon floor. Since it's an old road, the grade is not too steep. Nonetheless, it drops 750 feet in elevation in about 1.5 miles, which can get the heart rate up on the way back. The road is mostly slickrock at the upper end and turns to loose sand as you approach the canyon floor. This adds to the difficulty of climbing back out. Bring plenty of water.

You'll see the remains of historic ranching operations (fences, pipes, water troughs, etc.). You can also see the old 4WD road that drops into the canyon from the east rim, which was destroyed by a big storm in 1997 and then converted to a trail. When you reach the canyon floor, the trail turns right and follows the canyon bottom for 2 miles to the Great Gallery.

A ranger often stays much of the day at the Great Gallery to answer questions. Watch for short side trails to rock art sites. If you do miss them, you can catch them on the way back.

Rock art is extremely fragile and extremely precious, so don't touch any of the figures or disturb any artifacts found in the canyon. These are irreplaceable treasures. Crossing chain barriers placed around rock art by the NPS is prohibited, and this regulation is strictly enforced.

The rock art in Horseshoe Canyon is considered an example of the Barrier Canyon style, which dates back to the Late Archaic period from 2000 to 1000 BC. Later, the Ancestral Puebloan cultures left their marks in the canyon but apparently stayed only briefly. These early cultures were followed by modern cultures—cattle and sheep ranchers, oil prospectors, miners, and now park visitors. Throughout all this use, however, the special character of the canyon has been wonderfully preserved. All visitors have the responsibility to do their part to keep it that way.

The Great Gallery is the last of four interpretive stops the ranger makes. It's a sprawling rock art panel with large, intricate figures, both pictographs (painted figures) and

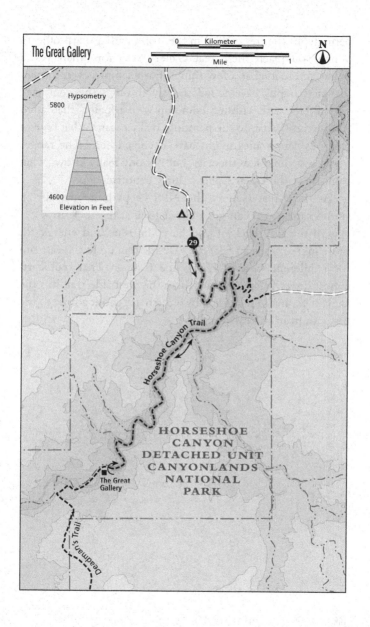

The Great Gallery

Hypsometry
5800
4600
Elevation in Feet

Horseshoe Canyon Trail

HORSESHOE
CANYON
DETACHED UNIT
CANYONLANDS
NATIONAL
PARK

The Great Gallery

Deadman's Trail

0   Kilometer   1

0   Mile   1

N

petroglyphs (figures etched in the stone with a sharp object). When you reach the Great Gallery, stop for lunch, rest a while, and marvel at a few things. For example, even though the pictographs have faded slightly through the centuries, how did the early cultures come up with a "paint" that lasted 3,000 years? What do the paintings really mean? What type of religious ceremonies might have occurred here? The ranger might toss out a few theories, but nobody really knows what went on at the Great Gallery thirty centuries ago.

At the Great Gallery, the NPS keeps binoculars in an ammo can so you can get a closer look at the rock art.

On the way back, if you have the time and energy for more hiking, you can take the east side trail up to the east rim for a different view of Horseshoe Canyon. That trail starts almost directly across from where the west side trail hits the canyon wash and is marked by a cairn. It's about a mile to the east rim from the canyon floor.

# 30 Happy Canyon

A nice day hike and a good choice for people who want to hike in the Maze District but don't have a 4WD vehicle.

**Start:** Trailhead at end of Happy Canyon Spur Road
**Distance:** 1.6 miles; out-and-back

**Maps:** Trails Illustrated Canyonlands National Park and USGS Gordon Flats and Clearwater Canyon

**Finding the trailhead:** From Hans Flat Ranger Station, drive 2.5 miles to the Panorama Point junction and take a right (south) onto Gordon Flats Road. After 12.1 miles, pass by the left turn to the Flint Trail and keep going straight for another 1.3 miles until you see the right-hand turn (west) to Happy Canyon Camp. Turn here and go 0.4 mile to the camp on your left. The rest of the road has been blocked because of severe erosion. You can park in the wide area where the road turns off to Happy Canyon Camp. GPS coordinates: N6 30.792' / W110 08.200'

## The Hike

This trail is actually an abandoned jeep road. That means it has a fairly easy grade, but the road has eroded and deteriorated to make the hike tougher than it normally would be. The trail doesn't receive much use, so you'll probably have a choice piece of the Canyonlands all to yourself.

After about a mile, the trail ends as it reaches the floor of Happy Canyon. From here, you can strike off in any direction to explore or set up your backpack camp. On the way down the trail, you get a sweeping view of the broad, flat Happy Canyon. You might want to take a few minutes on the way down to spot a few places to explore when you reach the end of the trail.

This hike is also a great choice for people who have only a two-wheel-drive vehicle. You can reach the end of the road without a 4WD vehicle, but there are a few rocky sections where you need to go very slowly and use great care. The NPS considers this an "overflow area" and recommends it when the Maze campsites fill up.

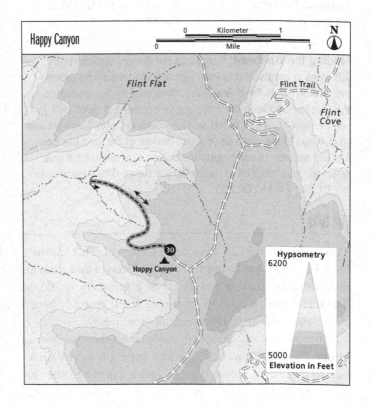

# 31 Spanish Bottom

A short, steep hike down to the Colorado River.

**Start:** Trailhead just before turn
to Doll House 1 Camp
**Distance:** 3 miles; out-and-back

**Maps:** Trails Illustrated Canyonlands National Park and USGS
Spanish Bottom

**Finding the trailhead:** From Hans Flat Ranger Station, drive
2.5 miles to the Panorama Point junction and take a right (south)
onto Gordon Flats Road. After 12.1 miles, turn left (east) and head
down the Flint Trail switchbacks for 2.8 miles to the Big Water Canyon Road, where you take a right (south). Follow this road along an
exposed ledge and down a steep dugway for 3.5 miles to a four-way
junction with Doll House Road. Turn left (northeast) and head for
the Doll House and Land of Standing Rocks. The map might show a
cutoff trail that looks like it can save some time, but this is deceptively incorrect. You can actually make faster time on the longer route
because of the excellent roads in this section. Once on Doll House
Road, stay on it for 20.8 miles to the Doll House Camps. When you
get to the Doll House area, the road forks, with Doll House 3 Camp
on the right and Doll House 1 and Doll House 2 camps on the left.
Take a left and the trailhead is on your left about 100 yards before
you turn again to Doll House 1 Camp. GPS coordinates: N9 18.350' /
W109 56.933'

## The Hike

The Spanish Bottom Trail drops steeply from the trailhead
all the way down to the Colorado River, hitting the river
just after the Colorado has absorbed the Green River. Even
though the trail drops about 1,100 feet in about a mile, it's
still the easiest way to get to the Colorado River from the

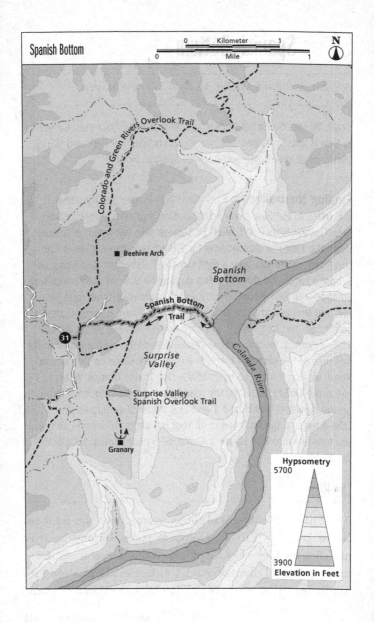

Spanish Bottom

0          Kilometer          1

0            Mile             1

N

Colorado and Green Rivers Overlook Trail

■ Beehive Arch

Spanish
Bottom

Spanish Bottom

Trail

31

Surprise
Valley

Colorado River

Surprise Valley
Spanish Overlook Trail

■ Granary

Hypsometry

5700

3900

Elevation in Feet

Doll House area. The well-constructed trail with frequent switchbacks partly mitigates the steepness. The trail is well defined and well marked the entire way.

The first quarter mile of the trail is nice and flat as it curves between the stunning sandstone towers of the Doll House. Then, shortly after you take a left at the junction with the Granary Trail, the Spanish Bottom Trail starts descending.

For most of the way down, you can see the large and extremely flat Spanish Bottom and the Colorado River flowing by it. You might see some campers, too, since this is a popular campsite for people floating the river. They like to camp here to gather their courage for the thunderous Cataract Canyon just around the bend in the river.

When you get to the bottom, take a break and relax for a while—and, of course, amass your strength for a steep climb up to the Doll House. The sharp incline makes this a great trail to hike in the coolish temperatures of the early morning or early evening.

# 32 The Granary

A short hike with some stunning scenery and cultural history.

**Start:** Trailhead just before turn to Doll House 1 Camp
**Distance:** 1.6 miles; loop

**Maps:** Trails Illustrated Canyonlands National Park and USGS Spanish Bottom

**Finding the trailhead:** From Hans Flat Ranger Station, drive 2.5 miles to the Panorama Point junction and take a right (south) onto Gordon Flats Road. After 12.1 miles, turn left (east) and head down the Flint Trail switchbacks for 2.8 miles to the Big Water Canyon Road, where you take a right (south). Follow this road along an exposed ledge and down a steep dugway for 3.5 miles to a four-way junction with Doll House Road. Turn left (northeast) and head for the Doll House and Land of Standing Rocks. The map might show a cutoff trail that looks like it can save some time, but this is deceptively incorrect. You can actually make faster time on the longer route because of the excellent roads in this section. Once on Doll House Road, stay on it for 20.8 miles to the Doll House camps. When you get to the Doll House area, the road forks, with Doll House 3 Camp on the right and Doll House 1 and Doll House 2 camps on the left. Take a left and the trailhead is on your left about 100 yards before you turn again to Doll House 1 Camp. GPS coordinates: N9 18.350' / W109 56.933'

## The Hike

The first part of the hike (which follows the same route as the Spanish Bottom Trail) is actually part of a small loop. After less than a half mile of flat, easy hiking through the Doll House towers, you reach a junction. Take a right (southwest)

and head to the Granary instead of dropping off the edge of the plateau to Spanish Bottom.

After another quarter mile of easy walking, you reach yet another junction, with the Granary Trail going to the left. The right fork takes you back to the trailhead, and you will take this path after you visit the Granary and see Surprise Valley.

Just before you reach the Granary, you see an overlook on your left only a few feet off the trail. From here, you get a spectacular vista of Surprise Valley, a classic graben and a gorgeous one at that. About another 100 yards up the trail is the Granary, a typical storage place used by the Ancestral Puebloans to hide grain for the lean winter months.

Canyonlands Natural History Association (CNHA) was established in 1967 as a not-for-profit organization to assist the scientific, educational, and visitor service efforts of the National Park Service (NPS), the Bureau of Land Management (BLM), and United States Forest Service (USFS).

CNHA's goals include enhancing each visitor's understanding and appreciation of public lands by providing a thorough selection of quality educational materials for sale in its bookstore outlets. A portion of CNHA's proceeds, including profit from this publication, is returned directly to our public land partners to fund their educational, research, and scientific programs. Bookstore sales support the agencies' programs in various ways, including free publications, outdoor education programs for local school districts, equipment, and supplies for ranger/naturalists, exhibits, and funds for research. Since our inception in 1967, CNHA has donated over $13 million to our public land partners.

# The Discovery Pool

CNHA established the Discovery Pool in 2006 to provide our federal partners with financial support for eligible scientific studies conducted within their administrative boundaries. The goals for use of the Discovery Pool grants are

- Encourage the scientific research that makes up the backbone of interpretive and educational programs, including resource management or protection surveys and monitoring.
- Provide matching funds that may assist federal partners in obtaining larger grants.
- Promote an understanding of the intricate cultural and natural resource complexities found on federally administered lands.

Since its inception, the CNHA Discovery Pool has awarded over $350,000 in grants to all of our federal partners! The wide range of projects includes but is not limited to the following studies:

- Goodman Point Archeological Project
- Bighorn Sheep Collaring
- Multi-Spectral Imaging of Rock Art in Canyonlands National Park
- Alpine Habitat Baseline Study
- Cedar Mesa Building Murals and Social Identities Project
- Paleontological Investigations of Comb Ridge, Utah

For a complete listing and description of all the Discovery Pool projects and for the guidelines to apply for a grant, please visit http://www.cnha.org/discovery-pool/. You can be a part of the Discovery Pool by becoming a Discovery member.

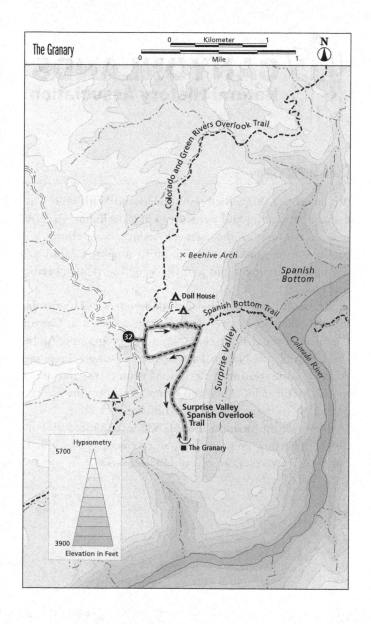

The Granary

0   Kilometer   1

0   Mile   1

N

Colorado and Green Rivers Overlook Trail

× Beehive Arch

Spanish Bottom

▲ Doll House

Spanish Bottom Trail

32

Surprise Valley

Colorado River

Surprise Valley Spanish Overlook Trail

■ The Granary

Hypsometry

5700

3900

Elevation in Feet

# CANYONLANDS
## Natural History Association

## CNHA Membership

People protect that which they understand. With visitor-use demands escalating and agency funding declining, CNHA's role in assisting in the agencies' educational efforts will continue to expand. Those wishing to support CNHA and our mission are invited to join the association's membership program.

Through your membership donation, CNHA is able to fund educational projects and programs such as Canyon Country Outdoor Education, Night Sky programs at Arches and Canyonlands National Parks, Junior Ranger Programs, Student Conservation Association volunteers, and much more. (Membership dues and other contributions are tax-deductible to the extent provided by law.)

For more information about CNHA, the Discovery Pool, our membership program, or our products, please visit us online at www.cnha.org or call (435) 259-6003.

# About the Author

Bill Schneider has spent a half-century hiking trails all across America. It all started in college in the late 1960s when he landed a job that paid him to hike, working on the trail crew in Glacier National Park. He spent the 1970s publishing the *Montana Outdoors* magazine for the Montana Department of Fish, Wildlife & Parks and covering as many miles of trails as possible on weekends and holidays. In 1979, Bill and his partner, Mike Sample, founded Falcon Publishing and gradually grew it for the next 20 years. Along the way, Bill wrote twenty-one books and hundreds of magazine articles on wildlife, outdoor recreation, and conservation issues. For 12 years, he taught classes on bicycling, backpacking, zero-impact camping, and hiking in bear country for the Yellowstone Institute, a nonprofit educational organization in Yellowstone National Park.

In 2000, Bill retired from his position as president of Falcon Publishing (now part of Rowman & Littlefield) after it had grown into the premier publisher of outdoor recreation guidebooks with more than 800 titles in print. During the early twenty-first century, he stayed in the publishing game for 6 more years by working as a consultant and acquisition editor for the Lyons Press and Falcon imprints and as Travel and Outdoor editor for *NewWest.Net*, a regional online magazine, where he wrote a weekly *Wild Bill* column devoted to what he called "outdoor politics."

He now lives in Helena, Montana, with his wife, Marnie, works as little as possible, and spends almost every day hiking, bicycling, or fishing.

**Books in Print by Bill Schneider**

*Backpacking Tips* (coauthor)

*Backpacker Magazine's Bear Country Behavior*

*Bear Aware, A Quick Reference Bear Country Survival Guide*

*Best Backpacking Vacations Northern Rockies*

*Best Easy Day Hikes Absaroka-Beartooth Wilderness*

*Best Easy Day Hikes Canyonlands and Arches*

*Best Easy Day Hikes Grand Teton*

*Best Easy Day Hikes Yellowstone*

*Best Hikes on the Continental Divide* (coauthor)

*Glacier National Park: Reflections*

*Hiking Canyonlands and Arches National Parks*

*Hiking Carlsbad Caverns and Guadalupe Mountains National Parks*

*Hiking Grand Teton National Park*

*Hiking Montana* (coauthor)

*Hiking Montana, Bozeman*

*Hiking the Absaroka-Beartooth Wilderness*

*Hiking Yellowstone National Park*

*The Tree Giants*

*Where the Grizzly Walks*

# THE TEN ESSENTIALS OF HIKING

**American Hiking Society**

Whether you plan to be gone for a couple of hours or several months, make sure to pack these items. Become familiar with these items and know how to use them.

### 1. Appropriate Footwear
Happy feet make for pleasant hiking. Think about traction, support, and protection when selecting well-fitting shoes or boots.

### 2. Navigation
While phones and GPS units are handy, they aren't always reliable in the backcountry; consider carrying a paper map and compass as a backup and know how to use them.

### 3. Water (and a way to purify it)
As a guideline, plan for half a liter of water per hour in moderate temperatures/terrain. Carry enough water for your trip and know where and how to treat water while you're out on the trail.

### 4. Food
Pack calorie-dense foods to help fuel your hike, and carry an extra portion in case you are out longer than expected.

### 5. Rain Gear & Dry-Fast Layers
The weatherman is not always right. Dress in layers to adjust to changing weather and activity levels. Wear moisture-wicking clothes and carry a warm hat.

### 6. Safety Items (light, fire, and a whistle)
Have means to start an emergency fire, signal for help, and see the trail and your map in the dark.

### 7. First Aid Kit
Supplies to treat illness or injury are only as helpful as your knowledge of how to use them. Take a class to gain the skills needed to administer first aid and CPR.

### 8. Knife or Multi-Tool
With countless uses, a multi-tool can help with gear repair and first aid.

### 9. Sun Protection
Sunscreen, sunglasses, and sun-protective clothing should be used in every season regardless of temperature or cloud cover.

### 10. Shelter
Protection from the elements in the event you are injured or stranded is necessary. A lightweight, inexpensive space blanket is a great option.

Find other helpful resources at AmericanHiking.org/hiking-resources.